Rick Steves'
SNAPSHOT

Stockholm

D0107554

CONTENTS

INTRODUCTION

This Snapshot guide, excerpted from my guidebook *Rick Steves' Scandinavia*, introduces you to Stockholm, the bustling capital of Sweden. With its modern buildings and dedication to green living, Stockholm has the feel of a gleaming metropolis, but it offers a satisfying blend of Old World charm and 21st-century tech. Start at its core with a stroll through the Old Town, Gamla Stan. Then visit the *Vasa* Museum with its 17th-century warship, the Nordic Museum covering five centuries of Swedish lifestyles, and Europe's original—and unsurpassed—open-air folk museum, Skansen. Indulge yourself in this city's aristocratic delights, including the Changing of the Guard at the Royal Palace and the elaborate *smörgåsbord* at the Grand Hotel. For a side-trip, visit Uppsala, a classic university town with a soaring cathedral. Then catch a boat and unwind among Sweden's rocky garden of more than 30,000 islands—Stockholm's Archipelago. Here in Stockholm's playground, you can count the pretty red cottages, go for a lazy stroll or bike ride, or relax on a sandy beach.

To help you have the best trip possible, I've included the following topics in this book:

• **Planning Your Time,** with advice on how to make the most of your limited time

• **Orientation,** including tourist information (abbreviated as TI), tips on public transportation, local tour options, and helpful hints

• **Sights** with ratings:

▲▲▲—Don't miss

▲▲—Try hard to see

▲—Worthwhile if you can make it

No rating—Worth knowing about

• **Sleeping** and **Eating,** with good-value recommendations in every price range

• **Connections,** with tips on trains, buses, and driving

Practicalities, near the end of this book, has information on money, phoning, hotel reservations, transportation, and more, plus Swedish survival phrases.

To travel smartly, read this little book in its entirety before you go. It's my hope that this guide will make your trip more meaningful and rewarding. Traveling like a temporary local, you'll get the absolute most out of every mile, minute, and dollar.

Ha en bra resa! Happy travels!
Rick Steves

SWEDEN

SWEDEN

Sverige

Scandinavia's heartland, Sweden is far bigger than Denmark and far flatter than Norway. This family-friendly land is home to IKEA, Volvo, WikiLeaks, ABBA, and long summer vacations at red-painted, white-trimmed summer cottages. Its capital, Stockholm, is Scandinavia's grandest city.

Once the capital of blond, Sweden is now home to a huge immigrant population. Sweden is committed to its peoples' safety and security, and proud of its success in creating a society with the lowest poverty rate in the world. Yet Sweden has thrown in its lot with the European Union, and locals debate whether to open their economy even further.

Swedes are often stereotyped as sex-crazed, which could not be farther from the truth. Several steamy films and film stars from the 1950s and 1960s stuck Sweden with the sexpot stereotype, which still reverberates among male tourists. Italians continue to travel up to Sweden looking for those bra-less, loose, and lascivious blondes... but the real story is that Sweden simply relaxed film censorship earlier than other European countries. Like other Scandi-

"Do you see the world as the world sees you?"

navians, Swedes are frank and open about sexuality. Sex education in schools is routine, living together before marriage is the norm (and has been common for centuries), and teenagers have easy access to condoms. But Swedes, who are the most unmarried people in the world, choose their partners carefully.

Before the year 2000, Sweden was a Lutheran state, with the Church of Sweden as its official church. Until 1996, Swedes automatically became members of the Lutheran Church at birth if one parent was Lutheran. Now you need to choose to join the church, and although the culture is nominally Lutheran, few people go to church regularly. While church is handy for Christmas, Easter,

marriages, and burials, most Swedes are more likely to find religion in nature, hiking in the vast forests or fishing in one of the thousands of lakes or rivers.

Sweden is almost 80 percent wilderness, and modern legislation incorporates an ancient common law called *allemans rätt*, which guarantees people the right to move freely through Sweden's natural scenery without asking the landowner for permission, as long as they behave responsibly. In summer, Swedes take advantage of the long days and warm evenings for festivals such as Midsummer (in late June) and crayfish parties in August. Many Swedes have a summer cottage—or know someone who has one—where they spend countless hours swimming, soaking up the sun, and devouring boxes of juicy strawberries.

While Denmark and Norway look westward to Britain and the Atlantic, Sweden has always faced east, across the Baltic Sea. As Vikings, Norwegians went west to Iceland, Greenland,

Sweden Almanac

Official Name: Konungariket Sverige—the Kingdom of Sweden—or simply Sweden.

Population: Sweden's 9.4 million people (about 50 per square mile) are mostly ethnically Swedish. Foreign-born and first-generation immigrants account for about 12 percent of the population and are primarily from Finland, the former Yugoslavia, and the Middle East. Sweden is also home to about 17,000 indigenous Sami people. Swedish is the dominant language, with most speaking English as well. While immigrants bring their various religions with them, ethnic Swedes who go to church tend to be Lutheran.

Latitude and Longitude: 62°N and 15°E, similar latitude to Canada's Northwest Territories.

Area: 174,000 square miles (a little bigger than California).

Geography: A chain of mountains divides Sweden from Norway on the Scandinavian Peninsula. Sweden's mostly forested landscape is flanked to the east by the Baltic Sea, which contributes to the temperate climate. Sweden also encompasses several islands, of which Gotland and Öland are the largest.

Biggest City: Sweden's capital city, Stockholm, has a population of 850,000; more than two million live in the metropolitan area.

Economy: Sweden has a $355 billion Gross Domestic Product and a per capita GDP of $39,100—similar to Canada's. Manufacturing, telecommunications, automobiles, and pharmaceuticals rank among its top industries, along with timber, hydropower, and iron ore. Because exports are a huge part of the Swedish economy, when the world's economy is down, so is Sweden's. The recent downturn has been

and America; Danes headed south to England, France, and the Mediterranean; and the Swedes went east into Russia. (The word "Russia" has Viking roots.) In the early Middle Ages, Swedes founded the Russian cities of Nizhny Novgorod and Kiev, and even served as royal guards in Constantinople (modern-day Istanbul). During the later Middle Ages, German settlers and traders strongly influenced Sweden's culture and language. By the 17th century, Sweden was a major European power, with one of the largest naval fleets in Europe and an empire extending around the Baltic, including Finland, Estonia, Latvia, and parts of Poland, Russia, and Germany. But by the early 19th century, Sweden's war-weary empire had shrunk. The country's current borders date from 1809.

During a massive wave of emigration from the 1860s to World War II, about a quarter of Sweden's people left for the Promised tough for Sweden—the value of the krona decreased, and many workers have moved to Norway in search of employment (Norway, with its oil wealth, is less affected by global economics). Eighty percent of Swedish workers belong to a labor union.

Currency: 6 Swedish kronor (kr, officially SEK) = about $1.

Government: King Carl XVI Gustav is the ceremonial head of Sweden's constitutional monarchy. Elected every four years, the 349-member Swedish Parliament (Riksdag) is currently led by Prime Minister Fredrik Reinfeldt of the conservative Moderate Party (elected in October 2006). The Economist magazine—which considered factors such as participation, impact of people on their government, and transparency—ranked Sweden by far the world's most democratic country (followed by the other Scandinavian countries and the Netherlands, with North Korea coming in last.)

Flag: The Swedish flag is blue with a yellow Scandinavian cross. The colors are derived from the Swedish coat of arms, with yellow symbolizing the generosity of the people and blue representing vigilance, truth, loyalty, perseverance, and justice.

The Average Swede: He or she is 42 years old, has 1.67 children, and will live to be 81.

Land—America. Many emigrants were farmers from the southern region of Småland. The museum in Växjö tells their story, as do the movies *The Emigrants* and *The New Land*, based on the series of books by Vilhelm Moberg.

The 20th century was good to Sweden. While other European countries were embroiled in the two World Wars, neutral Sweden grew stronger, finding a balance between the extremes of communism and the free market. After a recession hit in the early 1990s, and the collapse of Soviet communism reshaped the European political scene, some started to criticize Sweden's "middle way" as extreme and unworkable. But during the late 1990s and early 2000s, Sweden's economy improved, buoyed by a strong lineup of successful multinational companies. Volvo, Scania (trucks and machinery), Ikea, and Ericsson (the telecommunications giant) are leading the way in manufacturing, design, and technology.

SWEDEN

The recent economic downturn, however, has had its impact on Sweden's export-driven economy—its Saab car manufacturer filed for bankruptcy protection in the fall of 2011.

Sweden has come a long way when it comes to accepting immigrants. Less than a century ago, only Swedes who traveled overseas were likely to ever see people of different ethnicities. In 1927 a black man worked in a Stockholm gas station, and people journeyed from great distances to fill up their car there...just to get a look. (Business boomed and his job was secure.)

Since the 1960s, however, Sweden (like Denmark and Norway) has accepted many immigrants and refugees from southeastern Europe, the Middle East, and elsewhere. This praiseworthy humanitarian policy has dramatically—and sometimes painfully—diversified a formerly homogenous country. The suburbs of Rinkeby, Tensta, and Botkyrka are Stockholm's ethnic neighborhoods, and are worth visiting. Many of the service-industry workers you will meet have come to Sweden from elsewhere.

For great electronic fact sheets on everything in Swedish society from health care to its Sami people, see www.sweden.se.

Most Swedes speak English, but a few Swedish words are helpful. "Hello" is *"Hej"* (hey) and "Good-bye" is *"Hej då"* (hey doh). "Thank you" is *"Tack"* (tack), which can also double for "Please."

STOCKHOLM

If I had to call one European city home, it might be Stockholm. One-third water, one-third parks, one-third city, on the sea, surrounded by woods, bubbling with energy and history, Sweden's stunning capital is green, clean, and underrated.

The city is built on an archipelago of islands connected by bridges. Its location midway along the Baltic Sea made it a natural port, vital to the economy and security of the Swedish peninsula. In the 1500s, Stockholm became a political center when Gustav Vasa established the monarchy (1523). A century later, the expansionist King Gustavus Adolphus made it an influential European capital. The Industrial Revolution brought factories and a flood of farmers from the countryside. In the 20th century, the fuming smokestacks were replaced with steel-and-glass Modernist buildings housing high-tech workers and an expanding service sector.

Today, with more than two million people in the greater metropolitan area (one in five Swedes), Stockholm is Sweden's largest city, as well as its cultural, educational, and media center. It's also the country's most ethnically diverse city. Despite its size, Stockholm is committed to limiting its environmental footprint. Development is strictly monitored, and pollution-belching cars must pay a toll to enter the city.

For the visitor, Stockholm offers both old and new. Crawl through Europe's best-preserved old warship and relax on a scenic harbor boat tour. Browse the cobbles and antique shops of the lantern-lit Old Town. Take a trip back in time at Skansen, Europe's first and best open-air folk museum. Marvel at Stockholm's glittering City Hall, slick shopping malls, and art museums.

While progressive and sleek, Stockholm respects its heritage. In summer, military bands parade daily through the heart of town to the Royal Palace, announcing the Changing of the Guard and turning even the most dignified tourist into a scampering kid.

Planning Your Time

On a two- to three-week trip through Scandinavia, Stockholm is worth two days. For the busiest and best two-day plan, I'd suggest this:

Day 1: 10:00—See the *Vasa* warship (starting with video and tour); 12:00—Visit Nordic Museum; 13:00—Tour Skansen open-air museum and grab lunch there; 16:00—Ride boat to Nybroplan (summer only) and follow my self-guided walk through the modern city from Kungsträdgården; 18:30—Take Royal Canal boat tour (confirm last sailing time, no boats Jan-March).

Day 2: 10:00—Catch 1.25-hour bus tour from the Royal Opera House, or take the City Hall tour; 12:15—Catch the Changing of the Guard at the palace (13:15 on Sun); 13:00—Lunch on Stortorget; 14:00—Tour Royal Palace Museums and Armory and follow my Old Town self-guided walk; 18:30—Free evening (could take a harbor dinner cruise).

Day 3: With an extra day, add a cruise through the scenic island archipelago (easy to do from Stockholm), visit the royal palace at Drottningholm, take a side-trip to charming Uppsala, or spend more time in Stockholm (there's plenty left to do and experience).

Orientation to Stockholm

(area code: 08)

Greater Stockholm's two million residents live on 14 islands woven together by 54 bridges. Visitors need only concern themselves with these districts, most of which are islands:

• **Norrmalm** is downtown, with most of the hotels and shopping areas, and the combined train and bus station. Östermalm, to the east, is more residential.

• **Kungsholmen,** the island across from Norrmalm, is home to City Hall and several inviting lakefront eateries.

• **Gamla Stan** is the Old Town island of winding, lantern-lit streets, antiques shops, and classy cafés clustered around the Royal Palace.

• **Skeppsholmen** is the small, central, traffic-free park/island with the Museum of Modern Art and two fine youth hostels.

• **Djurgården** is the park island—Stockholm's wonderful green playground, with many of the city's top sights (bike rentals just over bridge as you enter island).

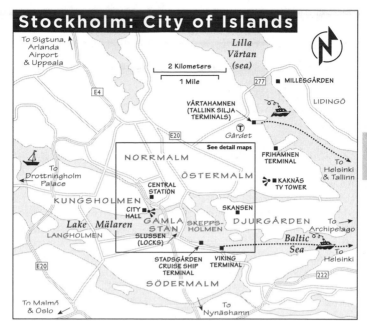

Stockholm: City of Islands

• **Södermalm,** just south of the other districts, is aptly called "Stockholm's Brooklyn" and is the primary setting for Stieg Larsson's Millennium novels. Apart from its fine views and some good eateries, this residential island may be of less interest to those on a quick visit. Its "SoFo" quarter is considered Stockholm's Greenwich Village, with a young, creative, trendy scene.

Tourist Information

Stockholm's **official TI** is across the street from the main entrance to the train station. The efficient staff provides free city maps, pamphlets on everything, Stockholm Cards (see below), transportation passes, day-trip and bus-tour information and tickets, and a room-booking service (75-kr fee for hotels, 25-kr/person fee for hostels). Avoid lines at the counter by looking up sightseeing details on one of the 10 user-friendly computer terminals (some with Internet access, 1 kr/minute). Check out their helpful "today's events" board and grab a copy of *What's On Stockholm,* a free monthly magazine with hours and directions for most sights, special event listings, and details on public transportation (Mon-Fri 9:00-19:00, Sat 10:00-17:00, Sun 10:00-16:00, shorter weekday hours in winter, Vasagatan 14, T-bana: T-Centralen, tel. 08/5082-8508, www.stockholm-town.com). The TI has placed computer terminals with tourist information in many hotel lobbies and at Stockholm's central train station, and TI kiosks open at cruise terminals when boats arrive. (The tourist booth in the Gallerian shopping mall is not an official TI.)

The **Airport Visitor Information Center,** a branch of the TI, is in Arlanda Airport's Terminal 5, where most international flights arrive. It offers many of the same services as the main TI (staffed daily 6:00-24:00, brochures available 24 hours, tel. 08/797-6000).

The **Stockholm Card,** a 24-hour pass for 425 kr, includes all public transit, free entry to almost every sight (75 attractions), some free or discounted tours, and a handy sightseeing handbook. An added bonus is the substantial pleasure of doing everything without considering the cost (many of Stockholm's sights are worth the time but not the money). The card pays for itself if you use public transportation and see Skansen, the *Vasa* Museum, and Drottningholm Palace. You can stretch it by entering Skansen on your 24th hour. A child's pass (age 7-17) costs about 60 percent less. The Stockholm Card also comes in 48-hour (550 kr) and 72-hour (650 kr) versions. Cards are sold at the main TI, airport TI, many hotels, hostels, larger subway stations, Pressbyrån newsstands, and at www.stockholmtown.com.

Arrival in Stockholm

By Train or Bus

Stockholm's adjacent train (Centralstation) and bus (City-terminalen) stations, at the southwestern edge of Norrmalm, are

a hive of services, shops, exchange desks, and people on the move. From the train station, the bus station is up the escalators from the main hall and across the street. Underground is the T-Centralen subway (T-bana) station, and taxi stands are outside. Those sailing to Finland or Estonia will find cruise-ship offices in the bus terminal, and can catch a shuttle bus to the port from here. The best way to connect the city and its airport is via the Arlanda Express shuttle train, which leaves from here (see next page).

Stockholm is building a new commuter rail line right beneath the T-Centralen station—expect lots of construction until at least 2014.

By Plane

Arlanda Airport: Stockholm's Arlanda Airport is 28 miles north of town (airport info: tel. 08/797-6000, www.arlanda.se). The airport TI (see "Airport Visitor Information Center," previous page) can advise you on getting into Stockholm and on your sightseeing plans.

The **airport shuttle train,** the Arlanda Express, is the fastest way to zip between the airport and the central train station (260 kr one-way, 490 kr round-trip, kids under 17 free with adult, covered by railpass; generally 4/hour—departing at :05, :20, :35, and :50 past the hour in each direction; even more frequent midday, 20-minute trip, has its own dedicated train station platform—follow signs to *Arlanda*, toll-free tel. 020-222-224, www.arlanda express.com). Buy your ticket either at the window near the track or from a ticket-vending machine, or pay an extra 50 kr to buy it on board. In summer and on weekends, a special fare lets two people travel for nearly half-price (two for 280 kr one-way, available daily mid-June-Aug, Sat-Sun year-round).

Airport shuttle buses (Flygbussarna) run between the airport and the train/bus stations (99 kr, 6/hour, 40 minutes, may take longer at rush hour, buy tickets from station kiosks or at airport TI, www.flygbussarna.se).

Taxis between the airport and the city center take about 30-40 minutes (about 500 kr, depends on company, look for price printed on side of cab). Establish the price first. Reputable taxis accept credit cards.

The **cheapest airport connection** is to take bus #583 from the airport to Märsta, then switch to the *pendeltåg* (suburban train, 2/hour), which goes to Stockholm's central station (72 kr, 1 hour total journey time, covered by Stockholm Card).

Skavsta Airport: Some discount airlines use Skavsta Airport, about 60 miles south of Stockholm (www.skavsta.se). Flygbussarna shuttle buses connect to the city (149 kr, timed to meet arriving flights, 80 minutes, www.flygbussarna.se).

By Boat

Most cruise ships dock at the Stadsgården terminal south of Stockholm's Old Town (Gamla Stan), but some use the Frihamnen terminal northwest of the city center. TI kiosks (with bus tickets, city guides, and maps) open at both terminals when ships arrive.

Stadsgården Terminal: It's about a 20-minute walk along the water to the Old Town and another 10 minutes to the city center. The nearby Viking Line shuttle bus connects with the train station (40 kr), as does public bus #53. The Slussen subway station is 15 minutes away on foot. Both the yellow hop-on, hop-off bus and the hop-on, hop-off boat serve Stadsgården. A taxi between the city center and the terminal costs about 100 kr.

Frihamnen Terminal: The blue hop-on, hop-off bus serves

Frihamnen. For public transit connections, follow the blue line painted on the sidewalk to the Frihamnen bus stop; buses #1 and #76 go to the city center. A taxi between Frihamnen and the city center costs about 200 kr.

By Car

Only a Swedish meatball would drive his car in Stockholm. Park it and use public transit instead. The TI has a *Parking in Stockholm* brochure. Those sailing to Finland or Estonia should ask about long-term parking at the terminal when reserving tickets; to minimize the risk of theft and vandalism, pay extra for the most secure parking garage.

Helpful Hints

Theft Alert: Even in Stockholm, when there are crowds, there are pickpockets (such as at the Royal Palace during the Changing of the Guard). Too-young-to-arrest teens—many from Eastern Europe—are hard for local police to control.

Emergency Assistance: In case of an emergency, dial 112.

Medical Help: For around-the-clock medical advice, call 08/320-100, then press 2 to get into the queue. The **C. W. Scheele** 24-hour pharmacy is near the train station at Klarabergsgatan 64 (tel. 08/454-8130).

Telephone Calls: For operator assistance, call 118-118. Numbers starting with 020 are toll-free. Numbers beginning with 070 and 073 are mobile phones—about triple the cost of a regular call. Some kiosks sell cheap international phone cards; look for shops serving Sweden's immigrant population (1 kr/minute calls to the US).

Internet Access: Some **7-Eleven** stores and **Pressbyrån** newsstands host "Sidewalk Express" Internet terminals. These are the best deal going. Just buy a card (29 kr/1.5 hours), remember your password, and you can pop into participating branches to log on. The card is shareable (but only one person at a time can use it) and valid for three days from your first log-in (branches open daily until late). There's a Sidewalk Express nook at the T-Centralen subway station and at the airport departure lounge (good if you have time to kill and an unexpired card).

Bookstore: The **Sweden Bookshop** has English versions of books by local writers, with a great selection of books by Astrid Lindgren (including her classic, *Pippi Långstrump,* a.k.a. *Pippi Longstocking*), Stieg Larsson's Millennium trilogy, local guidebooks, and tiny booklets on various aspects of Swedish life (Mon-Fri 10:00-18:00, closed Sat-Sun, at the bottom of the Palace Hill at Slottsbacken 10, tel. 08/453-7800, www .swedenbookshop.com).

Laundry: Tvättomaten is a rare find—the only independent laun-
derette in Stockholm (100 kr/load self-service, 200 kr/load
24-hour full-service—bring it in early and you can get it back
at the end of the day, open Mon-Fri 8:30-18:30, Sat 9:30-15:00,
closed Sun, across from Gustav Vasa church, Västmannagatan
61 on Odenplan, T-bana: Odenplan, tel. 08/346-480, www
.tvattomaten.com).

Bike Rental: Rent bikes and boats at **Djurgårdsbrons Sjöcafe,**
next to Djurgårdsbron bridge near the *Vasa* Museum
(bikes-60 kr/hour, 275 kr/day; canoes-125 kr/hour; handy
city cycle maps, May-Oct daily 9:00-21:00, closed in
bad weather, tel. 08/660-5757). It's ideally situated as a
springboard for a pleasant bike ride around the park-like
Djurgården island.

Stockholm's **City Bikes** program, similar to those in several other European cities, is another option for seeing this

bike-friendly town. Purchase
a 165-kr, three-day City Bike
card at the TI, at the SL Center
(Stockholm Transport) office at
Sergels Torg, or at many hotels
and hostels. The card allows
you to grab a bike from one of
the 80 City Bike racks around
the city. You must return it
within three hours (to any
rack), but if you want to keep
riding, just check out another
bike. You can do this over and over for three days (available
April-Oct only, www.citybikes.se/en).

Getting Around Stockholm

By Subway, Bus, and Tram: Stockholm's fine public transport
network (officially Storstockholms Lokaltrafik—but signed as *SL*)
includes subway (Tunnelbana—universally called "T-bana") and

bus systems, and a tram to the
sights at Djurgården. Special
passes take the bite out of the
cost. It's a spread-out city, so
most visitors will need public transport at some point
(transit info tel. 08/600-1000
and press * for English, www
.sl.se/english). The subway is
easy to figure out, but many
sights are better served by

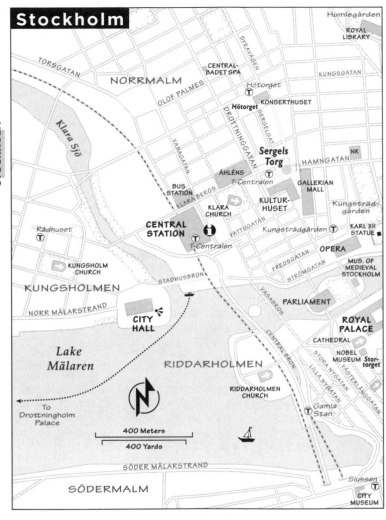

bus. The main lines are listed on the map in *What's On Stockholm*. A more detailed system map is posted around town and available free from subway ticket windows and SL info desks in main stations. Check out the modern public art in the subway (such as at Kungsträdgården station). Because of rail construction near the main train station, some T-bana stops in the vicinity may be temporarily closed: Look for orange information signs or ask the helpful staff.

A simple ticket takes you anywhere in town on either the subway or buses. There are four ticket options: a single ticket (36 kr), a book of eight tickets (200 kr), a 24-hour smartcard pass (135 kr),

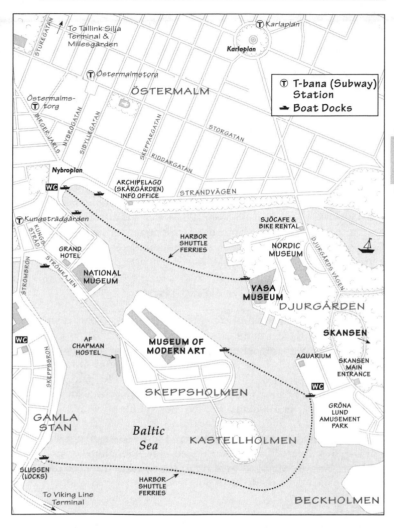

and a three-day smartcard pass (250 kr). Buy tickets from machines (US credit cards OK if you know your PIN code) or ticket booths (cash only) in underground stations, or at the Pressbyrån newsstands that are scattered throughout the city and inside almost every T-bana station. All SL ticket-sellers are clearly marked with a blue flag with the SL logo. Tickets are not sold on buses or trams—buy one before you board.

By Harbor Shuttle Ferry: In summer, ferries let you make a fun, practical, and scenic shortcut across the harbor to Djurgården island. Boats leave from Slussen (at the south end of Gamla Stan) every 10-20 minutes, docking near the Gröna Lund amusement park on Djurgården (May–mid-Sept only, 10-minute trip, 40 kr, tel. 08/679-5830, www.waxholmsbolaget.se). This ferry also stops near the Museum of Modern Art on Skeppsholmen Island. The Nybro ferry makes the five-minute journey from Nybroplan to Djurgården, landing next to the *Vasa* Museum (3/hour, June-Aug daily 10:00-20:00, check with TI for off-season schedule, 40 kr, tel. 08/1200-4000, www.stromma.se). The Hop-on, Hop-off Boat Tour (see next page) also connects many of these stops. While buses and trams run between the same points more frequently, this option gets you out onto the water.

By Taxi: Stockholm is a good taxi town if you get an honest cab (45-kr drop charge). I've been ripped off enough by cabs here to take only "Taxi Stockholm" cabs with the phone number (08/150-000) printed on the door. (Taxi Kurir is also reportedly honest: tel. 08/300-000.) Your hotel, restaurant, or museum can call a cab, which will generally arrive within minutes (you'll pay no extra charge—the meter starts when you hop in).

Tours in Stockholm

A company called **Stockholm Sightseeing** seems to have a lock on all city sightseeing tours, whether by bus, by boat, or on foot. Their website (www.stockholmsightseeing.com) covers the entire program, many of which are listed below. For more information on their tours, call 08/1200-4000. Tours can be paid for in advance online, or simply as you board. The Stockholm Card provides the following discounts: hop-on, hop-off bus—60 kr off the 260-kr price; 1.25-hour quickie bus tour—50 percent discount on late afternoon departures; Royal Canal Tour—40 kr off the 150-kr price; 50-minute Historic Canal boat tour—free; hop-on, hop-off boat—free in May and Sept only. The Stockholm Card does not cover the Under the Bridges boat tour or Old Town walk.

By Bus

Hop-on, Hop-off Bus Tour—Like hop-on, hop-off buses throughout Europe, Stockholm Sightseeing's topless double-decker buses make a 1.5-hour circuit of the city, linking all the essential places (the combo-ticket covers a total of 25 stops). The bus provides a convenient connection to sights from Skansen to City Hall, and the recorded commentary is good. The blue line tours the north part of town (and serves the Frihamnen cruise terminal); the yellow line covers the south end (and stops at the Stadsgården cruise terminal). A combo-ticket allows you to switch between lines (260 kr/24-hour combo-ticket, covers entry to Gröna Lund amusement park; May-Sept 2/hour daily 10:00-16:00, fewer in off-season, none mid-Jan-mid-Feb).

Quickie Orientation Bus Tour—Several different city bus tours leave from the Royal Opera House on Gustav Adolfs Torg. Stockholm Sightseeing's Stockholm Panorama tour provides a good overview (260 kr, 1.25 hours; daily at 10:00, 12:00, and 14:00; more frequent in summer).

By Boat

▲**City Boat Tours**—For a good floating look at Stockholm and a pleasant break, consider a sightseeing cruise. The handiest are

the Stockholm Sightseeing boats, which leave from Strömkajen, in front of the Grand Hotel, and from Nybroplan (each with recorded commentary). The **Royal Canal Tour** is short and informative (150 kr, 50 minutes, departs at :30 past each hour, generally daily May-Aug 10:30-18:30 but often as late as 19:30, April and Sept 10:30-16:30, Oct-Dec 10:30-13:30, none Jan-March). The nearly two-hour **Under the Bridges Tour** goes through two locks and under 15 bridges (200 kr, May-mid-Sept daily 10:00-16:00, June-Aug until 18:00, departures on the hour). A third option, the **Historical Canal Tour,** leaves from the Stadshusbron dock at City Hall (150 kr, 50 minutes, daily June-Aug 10:30-18:30, departs at :30 past each hour). You'll circle Kungsholmen island while learning about Stockholm's history from the early Industrial Age to modern times.

Hop-on, Hop-off Boat Tour—Stockholm is a city surrounded by water, making this boat option enjoyable and practical. The boat makes a small loop, stopping at key spots such as Djurgården (Skansen and *Vasa* Museum), Gamla Stan (near Slussen and again near Royal Palace), the Viking Line dock next to the cruise terminal at Stadsgården, and Nybroplan. Use the boat strictly as transport from Point A to Point B, or make the whole 50-minute, eight-stop loop and enjoy the recorded commentary (100-kr ticket good 24 hours, runs May-mid-Sept daily 1-2/hour roughly 10:00-17:00, pick up map for locations of boat stops).

By Foot

Old Town Walk—Stockholm Sightseeing offers a one-hour Old Town walk (150 kr, daily July-Aug at 11:30 and 13:30, leaves from Gustav Adolfs Torg, near the Royal Opera House).

Local Guides—To hire a private guide, call 08/5082-8508 (Mon-Fri 9:00-17:00, closed Sat-Sun) or visit www.guidestockholm.com. The standard rate is about 1,400 kr for up to a three-hour tour. **Marita Bergman** is a teacher and a licensed guide who enjoys taking around visitors during her school breaks (1,440 kr/half-day tour, tel. 08/5909-3931, mobile 073-511-9154, maritabergman@bred band.net). **Håkan Fränden** is also good (mobile 070-531-3379, hkan.frndn@telia.com).

Self-Guided Walks

This section includes two different walks to introduce you to Stockholm, both old (Gamla Stan) and new (the modern city).

▲▲Stockholm's Old Town (Gamla Stan)

Stockholm's historic island core is charming, photogenic, and full of antiques shops, street lanterns, painted ceilings, and surprises. Until the 1600s, all of Stockholm fit on Gamla Stan. Stockholm traded with other northern ports such as Amsterdam, Lübeck, and Tallinn. German culture influenced art, building styles, and even the language, turning Old Norse into modern Swedish. With its narrow alleys and stairways, Gamla Stan mixes poorly with cars and modern economies. Today, it's been given over to the Royal Palace and to the tourists—sometimes seemingly unaware that most of Stockholm's best attractions are elsewhere—who throng Gamla Stan's main drag, Västerlånggatan. While you could just happily wander, this quick walk gives meaning to Stockholm's Old Town.

• *Start at the base of Slottsbacken (the Palace Hill esplanade) leading up to the...*

Royal Palace: Check out the ❶ **statue of King Gustav III** gazing at the palace, which was built on the site of Stockholm's first castle (described later, under "Sights in Stockholm"). Gustav turned Stockholm from a dowdy Scandinavian port into a sophisticated European capital, modeled on buildings he'd seen in Paris, Vienna, and Berlin. Gustav loved the arts, and he founded the Royal Dramatic Theater and the Royal Opera in Stockholm. Ironically, he was assassinated at a masquerade ball at the Royal Opera House in 1792, inspiring Verdi's opera *Un Ballo in Maschera.*

Walk up the broad, cobbled boulevard. (The recommended Sweden Bookshop, with English books, is on the left near the bottom.) Partway up the hill, stop and scan the harbor. The grand building across the water is the National Museum, which is often mistaken for the palace. Beyond that, in the distance, is the fine row of buildings on Strandvägen street. Until the 1850s, this area was home to peasant shacks, but as Stockholm entered its grand stage, it was cleaned up and replaced by fine apartments, including some of the city's smartest addresses. (Tiger Woods shared a home here with his Swedish wife during their now-defunct marriage.)

STOCKHOLM

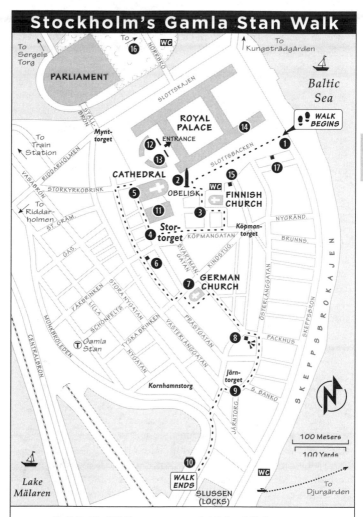

Stockholm's Gamla Stan Walk

Self-Guided Walk

1. King Gustav III Statue
2. Obelisk
3. Iron Boy Statue
4. Stortorget
5. Cathedral
6. Rune Stone
7. German Church
8. Viewpoint
9. Järntorget
10. Bridge & Lock

Additional Sights

11. Nobel Museum
12. Changing of the Guard
13. Palace Info Booth
14. Royal Armory
15. Royal Coin Cabinet & Swedish Economic Museum
16. To Museum of Medieval Stockholm
17. Sweden Bookshop

The TV tower—a major attraction back in the 1970s—stands tall in the distance. Turn to the palace facade on your left (finished in 1754, replacing one that burned in 1697). The niches are filled with Swedish bigwigs (literally) from the mid-18th century.

The ❷ **obelisk** honors Stockholm's merchant class for its support in a 1788 war against Russia. In front of the obelisk are tour buses (their drivers worried about parking cops) and a sand pit used for *boules*. The royal family took a liking to the French game during a Mediterranean vacation, and it's quite popular around town today. Behind the obelisk stands Storkyrkan, Stockholm's cathedral (which we'll visit later in this walk). From this angle, you see its Baroque facade, added to fit with the newer palace. Opposite the palace (orange building on left) is the Finnish church (Finska Kyrkan), which originated as the royal tennis hall. When the Protestant Reformation hit in 1527, church services could at last be said in the peoples' languages rather than Latin. Suddenly, each merchant community needed its own church. Finns worshipped here, the Germans built their church (coming up on this walk), and the Swedes got the cathedral.

Stroll behind the Finnish church into the shady churchyard where you'll find the fist-sized ❸ *Iron Boy*, the tiniest public statue

(out of about 600 statues) in Stockholm. Swedish grannies knit caps for him in the winter. Local legend says the statue honors the orphans who had to transfer cargo from sea ships to lake ships before Stockholm's locks were built. Some people rub his head for good luck (which the orphans didn't have). Others, likely needy when it comes to this gift, rub his head for wisdom. The artist says it's simply a self-portrait of himself as a child, sitting on his bed and gazing at the moon (notice the moonbeam-projecting light on the top of a pipe).

• *Continue through the yard, cross Trädgårdsgatan, go down the tiny lane to Köpmangatan (the medieval merchants' street, now popular with antiques dealers), turn right, and head for Stortorget, the old square.*

❹ **Stortorget, Stockholm's Oldest Square:** Colorful old buildings topped with gables line this square, which was the heart of medieval Stockholm (pop. 6,000 in 1400). This was where the many tangled lanes intersected, becoming the natural center for shopping and the town well. Today Stortorget is home to tourists, concerts, occasional demonstrators, and—in winter—Christmas shoppers at an outdoor market.

The grand building on the right is the **Stock Exchange.** It now houses the noble Nobel Museum (described later, under "Sights in

Stockholm"). On the immediate left is the social-services agency **Stockholms Stadsmission** (offering the cheapest and best lunch around at the recommended Grillska Huset).If you peek into one wing of the café, you'll get a fine look at the richly decorated ceilings characteristic of Gamla Stan in the 17th century. The exotic flowers and animals implied that the people who lived or worked here were worldly. Stockholms Stadsmission's trendy secondhand shop is just across the square at Trångsund 8. The town well is still a popular meeting point. Scan the fine old facades.

The site of the **Stockholm Bloodbath** of 1520, this square has a notorious history. During a Danish power grab, many of Stockholm's movers and shakers who had challenged Danish rule—Swedish aristocracy, leading merchants, and priests—were rounded up, brought here, and beheaded. Rivers of blood were said to have flowed through the streets. Legend holds that the 80 or so white stones in the fine red facade across the square symbolize the victims. (One victim's son escaped, went into hiding, and resurfaced to lead a Swedish revolt against the Danish rulers. Three years later, the Swedes elected that rebel, Gustav Vasa, as their first king. He went on to usher in a great period in Swedish history—the Swedish Renaissance.) This square long held the town's pillory.

• *At the far end of the square (under the finest gables), turn right and follow Trångsund toward the cathedral.*

❺ **Cathedral (Storkyrkan):** Just before the church, you'll see my personal phone booth (Rikstelefon) and the gate to the church-

yard—guarded by statues of Caution and Hope. Enter the yellow-brick church—Stockholm's oldest, from the 13th century (40 kr, free on Sun, daily mid-May-mid-Sept 9:00-18:00, until 16:00 off-season; worthwhile included English-language flier describes the interior). Signs explain events (busy with tours and services in summer).

The interior is cobbled with centuries-old **tombstones.** At one time, more than a thousand people were buried under the church. The tombstone of the Swedish reformer Olaus Petri is appropriately simple and appropriately located—under the pulpit. A witness to the Stockholm Bloodbath, Petri was nearly executed himself. He went on to befriend Gustav Vasa and guide him in Lutheranizing Sweden (and turning this cathedral from Catholic to Protestant).

Opposite the pulpit, find the **bronze plaque.** It recalls the 1925 Swedish-led ecumenical meeting of all Christian leaders—except the pope—that encouraged the Church to speak out against the type of evil that resulted in World War I's horrific death toll.

The **royal boxes** (between the pulpit and the altar) date from 1684. In front (on the left), *Saint George and the Dragon* (1489) is carved of oak and elk horn. To some, this symbolizes the Swedes' overcoming the evil Danes. In a broader sense, it's an inspiration to take up the struggle against even non-Danish evil. Regardless, it must be the gnarliest dragon's head in all of Europe.

Near the exit, a **painting** depicts Stockholm in the early 1500s, showing a walled city filling only today's Gamla Stan. It's a 1630 copy of the 1535 original. The strange sun and sky predicted big changes in Sweden—and as a matter of fact, that's what happened. Gustav Vasa brought on huge reforms in religion and beyond. (The copies show you the same painting, minus the glare.)

In June of 2010, this church hosted a royal wedding (Crown Princess Victoria, heir to the throne, married Daniel Westling, her personal trainer.) Imagine the pomp and circumstance as the nation's attention was drawn to this spot.

The plain door on the right leads to a free WC. The exit door next to the painting takes you into the kid-friendly churchyard (which was once the cemetery).

• *With your back to the church's front door, turn right and continue down Trångsund. At the next corner, go downhill on Storkyrkobrinken and take the first left on...*

Prästgatan Lane: Enjoy a quiet wander down this peaceful "Priests' Lane." (Västerlånggatan, the touristy drag, parallels this lane one block over—you can walk back up on it later.) As you stroll this 15th-century lane, look for hoists (merchants used these to lift goods into their attics), tie bolts (iron bars necessary to bind the timber beams of tall buildings together), small coal or wood hatches (for fuel delivery back in the good old days), and flaming gold phoenixes under red-crown medallions (telling fire-fighters which houses paid insurance and could be saved in case of fire—for example, #46). Like other Scandinavian cities, Stockholm was plagued by fire until it was  finally decreed that only stone, stucco, and brick construction (like you see here) would be allowed in the town center.

After two blocks (at Kåkbrinken), a cannon barrel on the corner (look down) guards a Viking-age ❻ **rune stone.** In case you can't read the old Nordic script, it says: "Torsten and Frogun erected this stone in memory of their son."

Continue farther down Prästgatan to Tyska Brinken and turn left. You will see the powerful brick steeple of the ❼ **German**

Church (Tyska Kyrkan, free, Mon-Sat 11:00-17:00, closed Sun except for services). Its carillon has played four times a day since 1666. Think of the days when German merchants worked here. Today, Germans come to Sweden not to run the economy, but to enjoy its pristine nature (which is progressively harder to find in their own crowded homeland). Sweden formally became a Lutheran country even before the northern part of Germany—making this the first German Lutheran church.

• *Wander through the churchyard and out the back. Exit right onto Svartmangatan and follow it to the right, ending at an iron railing overlooking Österlånggatan.*

❽ **Viewpoint:** From this perch, survey the street below to the left and right. Notice how it curves. This marks the old shoreline. In medieval times, piers stretched out like fingers into the harbor. Gradually, as land was reclaimed and developed, these piers were extended, becoming lanes leading to piers farther away. Behind you is a cute shop where elves can actually be seen making elves.

Walk right along Österlånggatan to ❾ **Järntorget**—a customs square in medieval times, and home of Sweden's first bank back in 1680 (the yellow building with the bars on the windows). A nearby Co-op Nara supermarket offers picnic fixings. From here, Västerlånggatan—the eating, shopping, and commercial pedestrian mall of Gamla Stan—leads back across the island. You'll be there in a minute, but first finish this walk by continuing out of the square (opposite where you entered) down Järntorgsgatan.

Walk out into the traffic hell and stop on the ❿ **bridge** above the canal. This area is called Slussen, named for the locks between the salt water of the Baltic Sea (to your left) and the fresh water of the huge Lake Mälaren (to your right). In fact, Stockholm exists because this is where Lake Mälaren meets the sea. Traders would sail their goods from far inland to this point, where they'd meet merchants who would ship the goods south to Europe. In the 13th century, the new Kingdom of Sweden needed revenue, and began levying duty taxes on all the iron, copper, and furs shipped through here. From the bridge, you may notice a current in the water, indicating that the weir has been lowered and water is spilling from Lake Mälaren (about two feet above sea level) into the sea. Today, the locks are nicknamed "the divorce lock" because this is where captains and first mates learn to communicate under pressure and the public eye.

Survey the view. Opposite Gamla Stan is the island of **Södermalm**—bohemian, youthful, artsy, and casual—with its popular Katarina viewing platform. Moored on the saltwater side are the cruise ships, which bring thousands of visitors into town each day during the season. Many of these boats are bound for Finland. The old steamer *Patricia* (see its two white masts, 200 or so yards toward Södermalm) is a local favorite for raucous dining and dancing. The towering white syringe is the Gröna Lund amusement park's free-fall ride. The revolving *Djurgården Färjan* sign marks the ferry that zips from here directly to Gröna Lund and Djurgården. The equestrian statue is Jean-Baptiste Bernadotte, the French nobleman invited to establish the current Swedish royal dynasty in the early 1800s.

You could catch bus #2, which heads back downtown (the stop is just beyond Bernadotte, next to the waterfront). But better yet, linger longer in Gamla Stan—day or night, it's a lively place to enjoy. Västerlånggatan, Gamla Stan's main commercial drag, is a festival of distractions that keeps most visitors from seeing the historic charms of Old Town—which you just did. Now you can window-shop and eat (see "Eating in Stockholm"). Or, if it's late, find some live music (see "Nightlife in Stockholm").

• *For more sightseeing, consider the other sights in Gamla Stan or at the Royal Palace (all described later, under "Sights in Stockholm"). If you continue back up Västerlånggatan (always going straight), you'll reach the Parliament building and cross the water back over onto Norrmalm (where the street becomes Drottninggatan). This pedestrian street leads back into Stockholm's modern, vibrant new town.*

From here it's also a 10-minute walk to Kungsträdgården, the starting point of my Modern City self-guided walk (described below). On the way there, you'll walk past the Royal Opera House and Gustav Adolfs Torg, with its imposing statue of Gustavus Adolphus. He was the king who established the Swedish empire. Considered by many the father of modern warfare for his innovative tactics, he was a Protestant hero of the Thirty Years' War.

Stockholm's Modern City

On this walk, we'll use the park called Kungsträdgården as a springboard to explore the modern center of Stockholm—a commercial zone designed to put the focus not on old kings and mementos of superpower days, but on shopping.

• *Find the statue of King Karl XII at the harbor end of the park.*

Kungsträdgården: Centuries ago, this "King's Garden" was the private kitchen garden of the king, where he grew his cabbage salad. Today, this downtown people-watching center, worth ▲, is considered Stockholm's living room, symbolizing the Swedes' freedom-loving spirit. While the English info board (near the harbor, 20 yards to the statue king's immediate right) describes the garden as a private royal domain, the nearby giant clump of elm trees reminds locals that it's the people who rule now. In the 1970s, demonstrators chained themselves to these trees to stop the building of an underground train station here. They prevailed, and today, locals enjoy the peaceful, breezy ambience of a teahouse instead. Watch the life-size game of chess and enjoy a summer concert at the bandstand. There's always something going on.

Kungsträdgården—surrounded by the harborfront and tour boats, the Royal Opera House, and, on the far side, a welcoming Volvo showroom (showing off the latest in Swedish car design), and the NK department store—is *the* place to feel Stockholm's pulse (but always ask first: *"Far jag kanna din puls?"*).

Kungsträdgården also throws huge parties. The Taste of Stockholm festival runs for a week in early June, when restaurateurs show off and bands entertain all day. Beer flows liberally—a rare public spectacle in Sweden.

The nearby Kungsträdgården T-bana station (on the side street called Arsenalsgaten) is famous for having the best art of any station in town. The man at the turnstile is generally friendly to tourists who ask *snälla rara* (snel-lah rar-rah; pretty please) for permission to nip down the escalator to see the far-out design, proving to the gullible that Stockholm sits upon a grand, ancient civilization.

• *Walk back to the park and stroll through Kungsträdgården up to Hamngatan street. Go left, and look for the. . .*

Gallerian Mall: Among this two-story world of shops, you'll find plenty of affordable little lunch bars, classy cafés for your *fika* (traditional Swedish coffee-and-bun break), and even a spa providing an oasis of relaxation for stressed-out shoppers.

• *Just beyond this huge mall, Hamngatan street leads to...*

Sergels Torg: This square, worth ▲, dominates the heart of modern Stockholm with its stark 1960s-era functionalist architec-

ture. The glassy tower in the middle of the fountain plaza is ugly in daylight but glows at night, symbolic of Sweden's haunting northern lights. The big, boxy, and glassy building overlooking the square is Stockholm's "culture center," the **Kulturhuset.** Inside, just past the welcoming info desk, you'll find a big model of the city.

There's a library, Internet café, chessboards, fun shops, fine art cinema, art exhibits, a venue for new bands, and a rooftop café with foreign newspapers and a grand view (Tue-Fri 11:00-18:00, Sat-Sun 11:00-18:00, closed Mon but retail shops stay open; tel. 08/5083-1508, www.kulturhuset.stockholm.se).

Stand in front of the Kulturhuset (across from the fountain) and survey the expansive square nicknamed "Plattan" (the platter). Everything around you dates from the 1960s and 1970s, when

Stockholm at a Glance

▲▲▲**Skansen** Europe's first and best open-air folk museum, with more than 150 old homes, churches, shops, and schools. **Hours:** Park—daily May-mid-June 10:00-19:00, mid-June-Aug 10:00-22:00, Sept 10:00-18:00, Oct and March-April 10:00-16:00, Nov-Feb 10:00-15:00; historical buildings—generally 11:00-15:00, June-Aug some until 19:00, most closed in winter. See page 37.

▲▲▲**Vasa Museum** Ill-fated 17th-century warship dredged from the sea floor, now the showpiece of an interesting museum. **Hours:** June-Aug daily 8:30-18:00; Sept-May daily 10:00-17:00, Wed until 20:00. See page 39.

▲▲▲**Archipelago** Mostly half-day cruises to Vaxholm and many other small island destinations. **Hours:** Several options per day in summer, some including a meal on board. See page 44.

▲▲**Military Parade and Changing of the Guard** Punchy daily pomp starting at Nybroplan and finishing at Royal Palace outer courtyard. **Hours:** Mid-May-mid-Sept Mon-Sat parade begins at 11:45 (reaches palace at 12:15), Sun at 12:45 (palace at 13:15); April-mid-May and mid-Sept-Oct Wed and Sat at 11:45 (palace at 12:15), Sun at 12:45 (palace at 13:15); Nov-March starts at palace Wed and Sat at 12:00, Sun at 13:00. See page 30.

▲▲**Royal Armory** A fine collection of ceremonial medieval royal armor, historic and modern royal garments, and carriages, in the Royal Palace. **Hours:** June-Aug daily 10:00-17:00; Sept-May Tue-Sun 11:00-17:00, Thu until 20:00, closed Mon. See page 31.

▲▲**City Hall** Gilt mosaic architectural jewel of Stockholm and site of Nobel Prize banquet, with tower offering the city's best views. **Hours:** Required tours daily generally June-Aug every 30 minutes 9:30-15:30, off-season hourly 10:00-15:00. See page 33.

▲▲**Nordic Museum** Danish Renaissance palace design and five fascinating centuries of traditional Swedish lifestyles. **Hours:** Daily 10:00-17:00, Wed until 20:00. See page 40.

▲▲**Drottningholm Palace** Resplendent 17th-century royal residence with a Baroque theater. **Hours:** May-Aug daily 10:00-16:30,

Sept daily 11:00-15:30, Oct-April Sat-Sun only 12:00-15:30, closed last two weeks of Dec. See page 42.

▲**Nobel Museum** Star-studded tribute to some of the world's most accomplished scientists, artists, economists, and politicians. **Hours:** Mid-May-mid-Sept Wed-Sun 10:00-17:00, Tue 10:00-20:00; off-season Wed-Sun 11:00-17:00, Tue 11:00-20:00; closed Mon year-round. See page 28.

▲**Royal Palace Museums** Complex of Swedish royal museums, the two best of which are the Royal Apartments and Royal Treasury. **Hours:** Mid-May-Sept daily 10:00-17:00; Oct-mid-May Tue-Sun 12:00-16:00, closed Mon. See page 32.

▲**Royal Coin Cabinet and Swedish Economic Museum** Europe's best look at the history of money, with a sweep through the evolution of the Swedish economy to boot. **Hours:** Daily 9:00-16:00. See page 33.

▲**Kungsträdgården** Stockholm's lively central square, with life-size chess games, concerts, and perpetual action. **Hours:** Always open. See page 24.

▲**Sergels Torg** Modern square with underground mall. **Hours:** Always open. See page 25.

▲**National Museum of Fine Arts** Convenient, crowd-free gallery with work of locals Larsson and Zorn, along with Rembrandt, Rubens, and Impressionists. **Hours:** June-Aug Wed-Sun 11:00-17:00, Tue 11:00-20:00, closed Mon; Sept-May Tue and Thu 11:00-20:00, Wed and Fri-Sun 11:00-17:00, closed Mon. See page 34.

▲**Thielska Galleriet** Enchanting waterside mansion with works of local artists Larsson, Zorn, and Munch. **Hours:** Daily 12:00-16:00. See page 41.

▲**Millesgården** Dramatic cliffside museum and grounds featuring works of Sweden's greatest sculptor, Carl Milles. **Hours:** May-Sept daily 11:00-17:00; Oct-April Tue-Sun 11:00-17:00, closed Mon. See page 41.

this formerly run-down area was reinvented as an urban "space of the future." In the 1980s, with no nearby residences, the desolate Plattan became the domain of junkies. Now the city is actively revitalizing it, and the Plattan is becoming a people-friendly heart of the commercial town. Designtorget (on the lower level) is a place for independent Swedish designers to market and sell their clever products. Perhaps you need a banana case?

Nearby are the major boutiques and department stores: Nordiska Kompaniet (NK), H&M, and Åhléns. The thriving pedestrian street **Sergelgatan** leads past the five uniform white towers you see beyond the fountain. These office towers, so modern in the 1960s, have gone from seeming hopelessly out-of-date to being considered "retro," and are now quite popular with young professionals.

• *Walk up Sergelgatan past the towers, enjoying the public art and people-watching, to the market at Hötorget.*

Hötorget: "Hötorget" means "Hay Market," but today its stalls feed people rather than horses. The adjacent indoor market, Hötorgshallen, is fun and fragrant. It dates from 1914 when, for hygienic reasons, the city forbade selling fish and meat outdoors. Carl Milles' statue of *Orpheus Emerging from the Underworld* (with seven sad muses) stands in front of the city concert hall (which hosts the annual Nobel Prize award ceremony). The concert house, from 1926, is Swedish Art Deco (a.k.a. "Swedish Grace"). The lobby (open through most of summer, 70-kr tours) still evokes Stockholm's Roaring Twenties.

Popping into the Hötorget T-bana station provides a fun glimpse at local urban design. Stockholm's subway system was inaugurated in the 1950s, and many stations are modern art installations in themselves.

• *Our walk ends here. For more shopping and an enjoyable pedestrian boulevard leading back into the Old Town, cut down a block to Drottninggatan and turn left. This busy drag leads straight out of the commercial district, passes the Parliament, then becomes the main street of Gamla Stan.*

Sights in Stockholm

Gamla Stan

The best of Gamla Stan is covered in my self-guided walk, earlier. But here are a few ways to extend your time in the Old Town.

▲**Nobel Museum (Nobelmuseet)**—Opened in 2001 for the 100-year anniversary of the Nobel Prize, this wonderful little

museum tells the story of the world's most prestigious prize. Stockholm-born Alfred Nobel was a great inventor, with more than 300 patents. His most famous invention: dynamite. Living in the late 1800s, Nobel was a man of his age. It was a time of great optimism, wild ideas, and grand projects. His dynamite enabled entire nations to blast their way into the modern age with canals, railroads, and tunnels. It made warfare much more destructive. And it also made Alfred Nobel a very wealthy man.

Wanting to leave a legacy that celebrated and supported people with great ideas, Alfred used his fortune to fund the Nobel Prize. Every year since 1901, laureates have been honored in the fields of physics, chemistry, medicine, literature, and peacemaking. Portraits of all 700-plus prizewinners hang from the ceiling—shuffling around the room like shirts at the dry cleaner's (miss your favorite, and he or she will come around again in three hours). Two video rooms run a continuous montage of quick programs (three-minute bios of various winners in one program, five-minute films celebrating various intellectual environments—from Cambridge to Parisian cafés—in the other). The Viennese-style Kafé Satir is the place to get creative with your coffee...and sample the famous Nobel ice cream. All Nobel laureates who visit the museum are asked to sign the bottom of a chair in the café. Turn yours over and see who warmed your chair. And don't miss the lockable hangers, to protect your fancy, furry winter coat. The Swedish Academy, which awards the Nobel Prize for literature each year, is upstairs.

Cost and Hours: 70 kr, free Tue after 17:00, audioguide-20 kr; open mid-May-mid-Sept Wed-Sun 10:00-17:00, Tue 10:00-20:00; off-season Wed-Sun 11:00-17:00, Tue 11:00-20:00; closed Mon year-round; free guided tours in English in summer Tue-Sat at 10:15, 11:15, 15:00, and 16:00, fewer off-season; on Stortorget in the center of Gamla Stan a block from the Royal Palace, tel. 08/5348-1800, www.nobelmuseum.se.

Parliament (Riksdaghuset)—For a firsthand look at Sweden's government, tour the Parliament buildings. It's also possible to watch the Parliament in session.

Cost and Hours: Free one-hour tours in English late June-Aug; usually Mon-Fri at 12:00, 13:00, 14:00, and 15:00; enter at Riksgatan 3a, call 08/786-4862 to confirm times, www.riksdagen.se.

Museum of Medieval Stockholm (Medeltidsmuseet)—This museum, recently renovated, provides a good look at medieval

Stockholm. When the government was digging a parking garage near the Parliament building in the 1970s, workers uncovered a major archaeological find: parts of the town wall which King Gustav Vasa built in the 1530s, as well as a churchyard. This underground museum preserves these discoveries and explains how Stockholm grew from a medieval village to a major city.

Cost and Hours: Free; Tue-Sun 12:00-17:00, Wed until 19:00; closed Mon; English audioguide, enter museum from park in front of Parliament, tel. 08/5083-1790, www.medeltidsmuseet .stockholm.se.

Nearby: The museum sits in **Strömparterren** park. With its café and Carl Milles statue of the *Sun Singer* greeting the day, it's a pleasant place for a sightseeing break (pay WC in park, free WC in museum).

Royal Palace (Kungliga Slottet)

Although the royal family beds down at Drottningholm, this complex in Gamla Stan is still the official royal residence. The palace, designed in Italian Baroque style, was completed in 1754 after a fire wiped out the previous palace. Today its exterior is undergoing a 20-year renovation—don't be surprised if parts are covered in scaffolding.

The Changing of the Guard and the awesome, can't-miss Royal Armory are the palace's highlights. The Royal Treasury is worth a look; the chapel is nice but no big deal; the Apartments of State are not much as far as palace rooms go; and you can skip Gustav III's Museum of Antiquities and the Museum of Three Crowns. The information booth in the semicircular courtyard (at the top, where the guard changes) gives out an explanatory brochure with a map marking the different entrances (main entrance is on the west side—away from the water—but the Royal Armory has a separate entrance). They also have a list of today's guided tours. In peak season, there are up to three different English tours a day (included in the admission)—allowing you to systematically cover nearly the entire complex. Since the palace is used for state functions, it is sometimes closed to tourists.

▲▲Military Parade and Changing of the Guard—Starting at Nybroplan, Stockholm's daily military parade marches over Norrbro bridge and up to the Royal Palace's outer courtyard, where the band plays and the guard changes.

The performance is fresh and spirited, because the soldiers are visiting

Stockholm just like you—and it's a chance for young soldiers from all over Sweden in every branch of the service to show their stuff

in the big city. Pick your place at the palace courtyard, where the band arrives at about 12:15 (13:15 on Sun). The best spot to stand is along the wall in the inner courtyard, near the palace information and ticket office. There are columns with wide pedestals for easy perching, as well as benches that people stand on to view the ceremony (arrive early). Generally, after the barking and goose-stepping formalities, the band shows off for an impressive 30-minute marching concert. Though the royal family now lives out of town at Drottningholm, the palace guards are for real. If the guard by the cannon in the semicircular courtyard looks a little lax, try wandering discreetly behind him.

STOCKHOLM

Cost and Hours: Free; mid-May-mid-Sept Mon-Sat parade begins at 11:45 (reaches palace at 12:15), Sun at 12:45 (palace at 13:15); April-mid-May and mid-Sept-Oct Wed and Sat at 11:45 (palace at 12:15), Sun at 12:45 (palace at 13:15); Nov-March starts at palace Wed and Sat at 12:00, Sun at 13:00. Royal appointments can disrupt the schedule; confirm times at TI. In summer, you might also catch the mounted guards (but they do not appear on a regular schedule).

▲▲**Royal Armory (Livrustkammaren)**—The oldest museum in Sweden is more than an armory and less than an armory. It displays impressive ceremonial royal armor (never used in battle), but there's a lot more to see. Everything is beautifully lit and displayed, and well-described in English and by the museum's evocative audioguide.

Cost and Hours: 75 kr; June-Aug daily 10:00-17:00; Sept-May Tue-Sun 11:00-17:00, Thu until 20:00, closed Mon; 20-kr audioguide is excellent—romantic couples can share it if they crank up the volume, information sheets in English available in most rooms; entrance at bottom of Slottsbacken at base of palace, tel. 08/5195-5546, www.livrustkammaren.se.

Touring the Museum: The first room is almost a shrine for Swedish visitors. It contains the clothes Gustavus Adolphus wore, and even the horse he was riding, when he was killed in the Thirty Years' War. The exquisite workmanship on the **ceremonial armor** in this room is a fine example of weaponry as an art form. The next room shows royal suits and gowns through the ages. The 1766 wedding dress of Queen Sofia is designed to cleverly show off its fabulously rich fabric (the dress seems even wider when compared to her 20-inch corseted waist). There are some modern royal dresses here as well. The royal children get a section for themselves, featuring a cradle that has rocked heirs to the throne since the 1650s; eventually it will leave the armory to rock the next royal offspring as well. It's fun to imagine little princes romping around their 600-room home with these toys. A century ago, one prince treasured his boxcar and loved playing cowboys and Indians.

The basement is a royal garage filled with **lavish coaches.** The highlight: a plush coronation coach made in France in about 1700 and shipped to Stockholm, ready to be assembled IKEA-style. It last rolled a king to his big day—with its eight fine horses and what was then the latest in suspension gear—in the mid-1800s. A display of royal luggage over the centuries makes it obvious that Swedish royalty didn't know how to pack light.

▲**Other Royal Palace Museums**—The four museums below can be accessed through the main entrance. Stockholm Card-holders can go straight into each museum, bypassing the ticket office.

Cost and Hours: 140-kr combo-ticket, otherwise 100 kr each, generally includes guided tour; mid-May-Sept daily 10:00-17:00; Oct-mid-May Tue-Sun 12:00-16:00, closed Mon; tel. 08/402-6130, www.royalcourt.se.

Royal Apartments: The stately palace exterior encloses 608 rooms (one more than Britain's Buckingham Palace) of glittering 18th-century Baroque and Rococo decor. Clearly the palace of Scandinavia's superpower, it's steeped in royal history. You'll walk the long halls through four sections: the Hall of State (with an exhibit of fancy state awards), the lavish Bernadotte Apartments (some fine Rococo interiors and portraits of the Bernadotte dynasty), the State Apartments (with rooms dating to the 1690s), and the Guest Apartments, where visiting heads of state still crash. Guided tours in English run daily in summer at 11:00 and 14:00 (45 minutes, off-season at 14:00 and 15:00).

Royal Treasury (Skattkammaren): Climbing down into the super-secure vault, you'll see 12 cases filled with fancy crowns, scepters, jeweled robes, and plenty of glittering gold. Nothing is explained, so pay for the flier or take the guided tour in English (May-Sept daily at 13:00, Oct-April Tue-Sun at 13:00).

Gustav III's Museum of Antiquities (Gustav III's Antik-museum): In the 1700s, Gustav III traveled through Italy and brought home an impressive gallery of classical Roman statues. These are displayed exactly as they were in the 1790s. This was a huge deal for those who had never been out of Sweden (closed mid-Sept-mid-May).

Museum of Three Crowns (Museum Tre Kronor): This museum shows off bits of the palace from before a devastating 1697 fire. It's basically just more old stuff, interesting only to real history buffs (guided tours in English at 16:00 in summer).

▲Royal Coin Cabinet and Swedish Economic Museum (Kungliga Myntkabinettet/Sveriges Ekonomiska Museum)—More than your typical royal coin collection, this is the best money museum I've seen in Europe. A fine exhibit tells the story of money from crude wampum to credit cards, and traces the development of the modern Swedish economy. Unfortunately, there aren't many English translations, which makes the included audioguide critical.

Cost and Hours: 60 kr, free on Mon, open daily 9:00-16:00, Slottsbacken 6, tel. 08/5195-5304, www.myntkabinettet.se.

Downtown Stockholm

Waterside Walk—Enjoy Stockholm's ever-expanding shoreline promenades. Tracing the downtown shoreline while dodging in-line skaters and ice-cream trolleys (rather than cars and buses), you can walk from Slussen across Gamla Stan, all the way to the good ship *Vasa* in Djurgården. Perhaps the best stretch is along waterfront Strandvägen street (from Nybroplan past weather-beaten old boats and fancy facades to Djurgården). As you stroll, keep in mind that there's free fishing in central Stockholm, and the harbor waters are restocked every spring with thousands of new fish. Locals tell of one lucky lad who pulled in an 80-pound salmon.

▲▲City Hall (Stadshuset)—The Stadshuset is an impressive mix of eight million red bricks, 19 million chips of gilt mosaic, and lots of Stockholm pride. While churches

dominate cities in southern Europe, in Scandinavian capitals, city halls seem to be the most impressive buildings, celebrating humanism and the ideal of people working together in community. Built in 1923, this is still a functioning city hall. The members of the city council—101 people (mostly women) representing the 850,000 people of Stockholm—are hobby legislators with regular day jobs. That's why they meet in the evening. One of Europe's finest public buildings and the site of the annual Nobel Prize banquet, City Hall is particularly enjoyable and worthwhile for its entertaining and required 50-minute tour.

Cost and Hours: 90 kr; English-only tours offered daily, generally June-Aug every 30 minutes 9:30-15:30, off-season hourly 10:00-15:00; call to confirm, 300 yards behind station, bus #3 or #62, tel. 08/5082-9059, www.stockholm.se/cityhall). City Hall's cafeteria, which you enter from the courtyard, serves complete lunches for 75 kr (Mon-Fri 11:00-14:00, closed Sat-Sun).

▲**City Hall Tower**—This 348-foot-tall tower (an elevator takes you halfway up) rewards those who make the climb with a grand city view. As you huff your way up, you'll come upon models of busts and statues that adorn City Hall and a huge, 25-foot-tall statue of St. Erik. Erik, the patron saint of Stockholm, was originally intended to be hoisted by cranes up through the middle of the tower to stand at its top. But plans changed, big Erik is forever parked halfway up the structure, and the tower's top is open for visitors to gather and enjoy the view. At the roof terrace, you'll find smaller statues of Erik, Klara, Maria Magdalena, and Nikolaus: patron saints facing their respective parishes. Finally, you'll find yourself in the company of the tower's nine bells, with Stockholm spreading out all around you.

Cost and Hours: 40 kr, daily June-Aug 9:00-17:00, May and Sept 9:00-16:00, closed Oct-April. As only 30 people at a time are allowed up into the tower, there's often a very long wait. If there's a long line, I'd skip it.

▲**Orientation Views**—For a bird's-eye perspective on this wonderful urban mix of water, parks, concrete, and people, consider these three viewpoints: **City Hall Tower** (described above; view from tower pictured above); **Kaknäs Tower** (at 500 feet, once the tallest building in Scandinavia; 45 kr, June-Aug daily 9:00-22:00, Sept-May daily 10:00-21:00 except Sun until 18:00; restaurant on 28th floor, east of downtown—bus #69 from Nybroplan or Sergels Torg, tel. 08/667-2105); and the **Katarina** viewing platform in Södermalm, near the Slussen T-bana stop. (The Katarina elevator is no longer working, but you can get to the platform via a pedestrian bridge from Mosebacke Torg, to the south.)

▲**National Museum of Fine Arts (Nationalmuseum)**—Though mediocre by European standards, this 200-year-old museum is small, central, and user-friendly. Highlights include several canvases by Rembrandt and Rubens, a fine group of Impressionist works, and a sizeable collection of Russian icons. Seek out the exquisite paintings by the Swedish artists Anders Zorn and Carl Larsson. An excellent audioguide describes the top works.

The Stockholm-born **Carl Larsson** (1853-1919) became very popular as the Swedish Norman Rockwell, chronicling the everyday family life of his own wife and brood of kids. In the large central entrance hall, his two vast, 900-square-foot murals celebrating Swedish history (above the grand staircase) are worth a close look. *The Return of the King* shows Gustav Vasa astride a white horse. After escaping the Stockholm Bloodbath and leading Sweden's revolt, he drove out the Danes and was elected Sweden's first king (1523). Now he marches his victorious troops across a drawbridge, as Stockholm's burghers bow and welcome him home. In *The Midwinter Sacrifice*, it's solstice eve, and Vikings are gathered at the pagan temple at Gamla Uppsala. Musicians blow the *lur* horns, a priest in white raises the ceremonial hammer of Thor, and another priest in red (with his back to us) holds a sacrificial knife. The Viking king arrives on his golden sled, rises from his throne, strips naked, gazes to the heavens, and prepares to sacrifice himself to the gods of winter, so that spring will return to feed his starving people.

The museum's middle floor is dedicated to **design;** one wing covers the 1500s to the 1800s, the other 1900-2000. With thoughtful English descriptions, this exhibit walks you through the evolution of modern Swedish design: gracefully engraved glass from the 1920s, works from the Stockholm Exhibition of 1930, industrial design of the 1940s, Scandinavian Design movement of the 1950s, plastic chairs from the 1960s, modern furniture from the 1980s, and the Swedish new simplicity from the 1990s.

Cost and Hours: 100 kr, can be more with special exhibits, audioguide-30 kr; June-Aug Wed-Sun 11:00-17:00, Tue 11:00-20:00, closed Mon; Sept-May Tue and Thu 11:00-20:00, Wed and Fri-Sun 11:00-17:00, closed Mon; Södra Blasieholmshamnen, T-bana: Kungsträdgården, tel. 08/5195-4310, www.national museum.se.

Museum of Modern Art (Moderna Museet)—This bright, cheery gallery on Skeppsholmen island is as far out as can be, with Picasso, Braque, Dalí, Matisse, and lots of goofy Dada art (such as *Urinal*), as well as more contemporary stuff. Don't miss the beloved *Goat with Tire*. The excellent and included audioguide makes modern art meaningful to visitors who wouldn't otherwise appreciate it.

Cost and Hours: 80 kr, Tue 10:00-20:00, Wed-Sun 10:00-18:00, closed Mon, fine bookstore, harborview café, T-bana: Kungsträdgården plus 10-minute walk, or take bus #65, tel. 08/5195-5200, www.modernamuseet.se.

▲**Swedish Massage, Spa, and Sauna**—To treat yourself to a Swedish spa experience—maybe with an authentic "Swedish massage"—head for the elegant circa-1900 **CentralBadet Spa.**

Once in a Millennium: Stieg Larsson's Stockholm

With nearly 50 million copies of Stieg Larsson's Millennium trilogy of novels in circulation—and a high-powered Hollywood version of the first installment, *The Girl with the Dragon Tattoo*, in movie theaters, Stockholm has a new breed of tourist. Fans of Larsson's punked-out computer hacker heroine Lisbeth Salander and jaded journalist hero Mikael Blomkvist are stalking the city's neighborhoods, particularly Södermalm, just south of the Old Town.

Stockholm's geography is key to Larsson's crime thrillers: Most of the good guys live and work in the formerly working-class Södermalm, while many of the villains hail from tony neighborhoods near Parliament and City Hall, across the water.

If you come looking for Lisbeth or Mikael, the best place to start is the **City of Stockholm Museum** in Södermalm, near the Slussen T-bana stop (free, Tue-Sun 11:00-17:00, Thu until 20:00, closed Mon, Ryssgården, tel. 08/5083-1620, www.stadsmuseum.stockholm.se). The museum hosts a display of Larsson artifacts, including a reconstruction of Mikael Blomkvist's office at *Millennium* magazine, and offers Millennium walking tours in English (120 kr, Wed at 18:00, Sat at 11:30) and a Millennium sights map (40 kr).

A few blocks from the museum is the site of the fictional *Millennium* offices, above the Greenpeace headquarters at the corner of Götgatan and Hökens Gata (really it's just apartments). Two real businesses in Södermalm figure prominently in the trilogy: **Kvarnen,** an old-style pub where Lisbeth hangs out with an all-girl punk band (Tjärhovsgatan 4, near the Medborgarplastsen T-bana stop); and the **Mellqvist café** (Hornsgatan 78, near the Hornstull T-bana stop), where the love-struck Lisbeth sees Mikael kiss his mistress.

Admission includes entry to an extensive gym, "bubblepool," sauna, steam room, and an elegant Art Nouveau pool. A classic massage (50 minutes) costs 650 kr—you don't have to pay the entry fee if that's all you want. Reservations are smart. If you won't make it to Finland, enjoy a sauna here. There are two saunas—one mixed, one not. Bring your towel into the sauna—not for modesty, but for hygiene (to separate your body from the bench). The steam room is mixed; bring two towels (one for modesty and the other to sit on). The pool is more for floating than for jumping and splashing. The leafy courtyard restaurant is a relaxing place to enjoy affordable, healthy, and light meals.

Cost and Hours: 180 kr, increases to 220 kr Fri-Sun, towels and robes available for rent; Mon-Sat 6:00-21:00, Sun 8:00-18:00, last entry one hour before closing, closed Sun-Mon July-Aug; ages 18 and up, Drottninggatan 88, 10 minutes up from Sergels Torg, tel. 08/5452-1300, tel. 08/5452-1313, www.centralbadet.se.

Djurgården

Four hundred years ago, Djurgården was the king's hunting ground. Now this entire lush island is Stockholm's fun center, protected as a national park. It still has a smattering of animal life among its biking paths, picnicking local families, art galleries, and various amusements. Of the three great sights on the island, the Vasa and Nordic museums are neighbors, and Skansen is a 10-minute walk away (or hop on any bus—they come every couple of minutes). To get around more easily, consider renting a bike as you enter the island.

Getting There: Take tram #7 from Sergels Torg (the stop is right under the highway overpass) and get off at the Nordic Museum (also for the *Vasa* Museum), or continue on to the Skansen stop. In summer, you can take a ferry from Nybroplan or Slussen (see "Getting Around Stockholm," earlier). Walkers can enjoy the harborside Strandvägen promenade, which leads from Nybroplan directly to the island.

▲▲▲Skansen

This is Europe's original open-air folk museum, founded in 1891. It's a huge park gathering more than 150 historic buildings (homes,

churches, shops, and schoolhouses) transplanted from all corners of Sweden.

Skansen was the first in what became a Europe-wide movement to preserve traditional architecture in open-air museums. Other languages have even borrowed the Swedish term "Skansen" (which originally meant "the Fort") to describe an "open-air museum." Today, tourists still explore this Swedish-culture-on-a-lazy-Susan, seeing folk crafts in action and wonderfully furnished old interiors. While it's lively June through August before about 17:00, at other times of the year it can seem pretty dead.

In "Old Stockholm" (top of the escalator), shoemakers, potters, and glassblowers are busy doing their traditional thing (daily 10:00-17:00) in a re-created Old World Stockholm. The rest of Sweden spreads out from Old Stockholm. Northern Swedish culture and architecture is in the north (top of park map), and southern Sweden's in the south (bottom of map).

STOCKHOLM

Stockholm's Djurgården

Take advantage of the free map, and consider the 50-kr museum guidebook. With the book, you'll understand each building you duck into and even learn about the Nordic animals awaiting you in the zoo. Check the live crafts schedule at the information stand by the main entrance beneath the escalator to make a smart Skansen plan. Guides throughout the park are happy to answer your questions—but only if you ask them. The old houses come alive when you take the initiative to get information.

Kids love Skansen, where they can ride a life-size wooden *Dala*-horse and stare down a hedgehog, visit Lill' Skansen (a children's zoo), and take a mini-train or pony ride.

Cost and Hours: 120 kr (less in winter); park open daily May–mid-June 10:00-19:00, mid-June-Aug 10:00-22:00, Sept 10:00-18:00, Oct and March-April 10:00-16:00, Nov-Feb 10:00-15:00; historical buildings generally open 11:00-15:00, June-Aug some until 19:00, most closed in winter. Check their excellent website for "What's Happening at Skansen" during your visit (www.skansen .se) or call 08/442-8000 (press 1 for a live operator). Gröna Lund, Stockholm's amusement park, is across the street (described later).

Music: Skansen does great music in summer. There's fiddling (30-minute performances June-Aug Tue-Fri at 18:15), folk-dancing (June-Aug Tue-Fri at 19:00, also Sat-Sun at 16:00), and public dancing to live bands (Mon-Sat from 20:00, call for that evening's theme—big band, modern, ballroom, folk).

Eating at Skansen: While Skansen's main restaurant, **Solliden,** serves a big *smörgåsbord* lunch in a grand blue-and-white room (310 kr, daily 12:00-16:00 in summer), and the adjacent **Ekorren** cafeteria offers less-expensive self-service lunches with a view (100-kr daily specials; in summer daily 11:00-19:00, off-season 10:00-16:00), the most memorable meals are at the small folk food court on the main square, **Bollnastorget.** Here, among the duck-filled lakes, frolicking families, and peacenik local toddlers who don't bump on the bumper cars, kiosks dish up "Sami slow food" (smoked reindeer), waffles, hot dogs, and more. There are lots of picnic benches—Skansen encourages **picnicking.** (A small grocery store is tucked away across the street and a bit to the left of the main entrance.) The old-time **Stora Gungan Krog,** in Old Stockholm at the top of the escalator, is a cozy inn; their freshly baked cakes will tempt you (80-160-kr indoor or outdoor lunches—meat, fish, or veggie—with a salad-and-cracker bar, daily 10:00-20:00, until 15:00 in winter).

Aquarium: Admission to the aquarium is the only thing not covered on your Skansen ticket, but it is covered by the Stockholm Card (90 kr; June-Aug daily 10:00-18.00, Sept-May Tue-Sun 10:00-16:30, closed Mon; tel. 08/660-1082, www.aquaria.se).

▲▲▲*Vasa* Museum (Vasamuseet)

Stockholm turned a titanic flop into one of Europe's great sightseeing attractions. The glamorous but unseaworthy warship *Vasa*—top-heavy with an extra cannon deck—sank 20 minutes

into her 1628 maiden voyage when a breeze caught the sails and blew her over. After 333 years at the bottom of Stockholm's harbor, she rose again from the deep with the help of marine archaeologists. Rediscovered in 1956 and raised in 1961, this Edsel of the sea is today the best-preserved ship of its age anywhere—housed since 1990 in a brilliant museum. The masts perched atop the roof—best seen from a distance—show the actual height of the ship.

The *Vasa*, while not quite the biggest ship in the world, had the most firepower, with two fearsome decks of cannons. The 500 carved wooden statues draping the ship—once painted in bright colors—are all symbolic of the king's power. The 10-foot lion on the magnificent prow is a reminder that Europe considered the Swedish King Gustavus Adolphus the "Lion from the North." With this great ship, Sweden was preparing to establish its empire and become more engaged in European power politics.

Painstakingly restored, 95 percent of the wood is original (modern bits are the brighter and smoother planks). Displays are well-described in English. Learn about the ship's rules (bread can't be older than eight years), why it sank (heavy bread?), how it's pre-served (the ship, not the bread), and so on.

Cost and Hours: 110 kr, includes video and tour; June-Aug daily 8:30-18:00; Sept-May daily 10:00-17:00, Wed until 20:00; Galärvarvet, Djurgården, tel. 08/5195-4800, www.vasamuseet.se.

Getting There: The *Vasa* is on the waterfront immediately behind the stately brick Nordic Museum (described below), a 10-minute walk from Skansen. Or you can take tram #7 from downtown. The museum also has a good café inside. To get from the Nordic Museum to the *Vasa* Museum, face the Nordic Museum and walk around to the right (going left takes you into a big dead-end parking lot).

Sightseeing Strategy: For a thorough visit, plan on spend-ing at least an hour: Watch the 17-minute video, take the free 25-minute tour (in either order), then explore the boat and wan-der through the various exhibits. From June through August, the English-subtitled video generally runs at the top of the hour (last movie at 17:00), with English tours at :30 past each hour beginning at 9:30 (last tour departs at 16:30, fewer tours off-season, call for times).

▲▲Nordic Museum (Nordiska Museet)

Built to look like a Danish Renaissance palace, this museum offers a fascinating peek at 500 years of traditional Swedish lifestyles. It's arguably more informative than Skansen. Take time to let the excellent, included audioguide enliven the exhibits. Carl Milles' huge painted-wood statue of Gustav Vasa, father of modern Sweden, overlooks the main gallery.

Highlights are on the top two floors. The middle floor (level 3) holds the *Traditions* exhibit (showing and describing each old-time celebration of the Swedish year) and a section of exquisite table settings, and fancy fashions from the 18th through the 20th centu-ries. The top floor (level 4) has an extensive Sami (Lapp) collection, old furniture, and an exhibit showing Swedish living rooms over the last century; it provides an insightful look at today's Swedes, including an intimate peek at modern bedrooms (match photos of the owners with the various rooms).

Cost and Hours: 80 kr, free Wed evenings off-season; daily 10:00-17:00, Wed until 20:00; Djurgårdsvägen 6-16, at Djurgårdsbron, tram #7 from downtown, tel. 08/5195-6000, www .nordiskamuseet.se.

Other Djurgården Sights

Gröna Lund—Stockholm's venerable and lowbrow Tivoli-type amusement park still packs in the local families and teens on cheap dates. It's a busy venue for local pop concerts.

Cost and Hours: 90 kr, May-Sept daily 12:00-23:00, closed off-season, www.gronalund.com.

▲**Thielska Galleriet**—If you liked the Larsson and Zorn art in the National Gallery, and/or if you're a Munch fan, this charming mansion on the water at the far end of the Djurgården park is worth the trip.

Cost and Hours: 80 kr, daily 12:00-16:00, bus #69—not #69K—from downtown, tel. 08/662-5884, www.thielska-galleriet .se.

▲**Biking the Garden Island**—In all of Stockholm, Djurgården is the natural place to enjoy a bike ride. There's a good and reasonably priced bike-rental place just over the bridge as you enter the island, and a world of park-like paths and lanes with harbor vistas to enjoy.

Outer Stockholm

▲**Millesgården**—The villa and garden of Carl Milles is a veritable forest of statues by Sweden's greatest sculptor. Millesgården is dramatically situated on a bluff overlooking the harbor in Stockholm's upper-class suburb of Lidingö. While the art is engaging and enjoyable, even the curators have little to say about it from an interpretation point of view—so your visit is basically without guidance. But in Milles' house, which dates from the 1920s, you can see his north-lit studio and get a sense of his creative genius.

Carl Milles spent much of his career living in Michigan. But he's buried here at his villa, where he lived and worked for 20 years, lovingly designing this sculpture garden for the public. Milles wanted his art to be displayed on pedestals... to be seen "as if silhouettes against the sky." His subjects—often Greek mythological figures such as Pegasus or Poseidon—stand out as if the sky was a blank paper. Yet unlike silhouettes, Milles' images can be enjoyed from many angles. And Milles liked to enliven his sculptures by incorporating water features into his figures. *Hand of God,* perhaps his most famous work, gives insight into Milles' belief that when the artist created, he was—in a way—divinely inspired.

Cost and Hours: 95 kr, 30-kr English booklet explains the art; May-Sept daily 11:00-17:00; Oct-April Tue-Sun 11:00-17:00, closed Mon; restaurant and café, tel. 08/446-7590, www.milles garden.se.

Getting There: Catch the T-bana to Ropsten, then take bus #207 to within a five-minute walk of the museum.

▲▲**Drottningholm Palace (Drottningholms Slott)**—The queen's 17th-century summer castle and current royal residence has

been called "Sweden's Versailles." Touring the palace, you'll see art that makes the point that Sweden's royalty is divine and belongs with the gods. You can walk the two floors on your own, but with no explanations or audioguides, it makes sense to take the included guided tour.

Cost and Hours: 80 kr, May-Aug daily 10:00-16:30, Sept daily 11:00-15:30, Oct-April Sat-Sun only 12:00-15:30, closed last two weeks of Dec; free-with-admission palace tours in English are offered May-Aug usually at 10:00, 12:00, 14:00, and 16:00; fewer tours off-season; tel. 08/402-6280, www.royalcourt.se.

Services: There is no WC in the palace. The closest WC is a three-minute walk from the entrance, near the café and boat dock. The café serves light meals, and taxis usually wait nearby.

Getting There: Reach the palace via a relaxing one-hour boat ride (120 kr one-way, 165 kr round-trip, 125 kr round-trip

with Stockholm Card, departs from Stadhusbron across from City Hall on the hour through the day, tel. 08/1200-4000), or take the T-bana to Brommaplan, where you can catch any #300-series bus to Drottningholm (54 kr one-way, 30 minutes from city center).

Consider approaching by water (as the royals traditionally did) and then returning by bus and T-bana (as a commoner).

Touring the Palace: You'll see two floors of lavish rooms, where Sweden's royalty did their best to live in the style of Europe's divine monarchs. While rarely absolute rulers, Sweden's royals long struggled with stubborn parliaments. Perhaps this made the propaganda value of the palace decor even more important. Portraits and busts legitimize the royal family by connecting the Swedish blue bloods with Roman emperors, medieval kings, and Europe's great royal families. The portraits you'll see of France's Louis XVI and Russia's Catherine the Great are reminders that Sweden's royalty was related to or tightly networked with the European dynasties.

The king's bedroom looks like (and was) more of a theater than a place for sleeping. In the style of the French monarchs, this is where the ceremonial tucking-in and dressing of the king would take place. The Room of War—with kings, generals, battle scenes, and bugle-like candleholders—is from the time when Sweden was a superpower (1600-1750). The murals commemorate a victory over the Danes: It's said Swedish kings enjoyed taking the Danish ambassador here.

Of course, today's monarchs are figureheads ruled by a constitution. The royal family makes a point to be accessible and as "normal" as royalty can be. King Carl XVI Gustaf (b. 1946)—whose main job is handing out Nobel Prizes once a year—is a car nut who talks openly about his dyslexia. He was the first Swedish king not to be crowned "by the grace of God." The popular Queen Silvia is a businessman's daughter. At their 1976 wedding festivities, she was serenaded by ABBA singing "Dancing Queen." Their daughter and heir to the throne, Crown Princess Victoria, studied political science at Yale and interned with Sweden's European Union delegation. In 2010 she married gym owner Daniel Westling—the first royal wedding in Sweden since her parents' marriage. Swedes await the birth of Victoria and Daniel's first child in March of 2012. Boy or girl, their child automatically becomes the next heir to the throne.

Drottningholm Court Theater (Drottningholms Slottsteater): This 18th-century theater somehow survived the ages—complete with its instruments, sound-effects machines, and stage sets. It's one of two such theaters remaining in Europe (the other is in Český Krumlov, Czech Republic). Visit it on a 30-minute guided tour, offered at the top of the hour (90 kr, May-Aug 11:00-16:30, Sept 12:00-15:30, no tours off-season, tel. 08/759-0406), or check their schedule for the rare opportunity to see perfectly authentic operas (about 25 performances each summer). Tickets for this popular time-travel musical and theatrical experience cost 275-895 kr and go on sale each March; purchase online or by phone or fax (see www.dtm.se).

Sigtuna—This town, an old-time lakeside jumble of wooden houses and waffle shops, presents a fluffy, stereotyped version of Sweden in the olden days. You'll see a medieval lane lined with colorful tourist boutiques, cafés, a romantic park, waterfront promenade, old town hall, and rune stones. The TI can help you get oriented (tel. 08/5948-0650, http://sal.sigtuna.se/turism). If traveling by car to Uppsala or Oslo, Sigtuna is a short detour, good for a browse and an ice-cream cone, but little more. By public transport, it's probably not worth the tedious one-hour trip out (take the *pendeltåg* suburban train from Stockholm to Märsta and then change to bus #570).

▲▲▲Archipelago (Skärgården)—Some of Europe's most scenic islands (thousands of them) stretch 80 miles from Stockholm

out to the open Baltic Sea. If you cruise to Finland, you'll get a good dose of this island beauty. Otherwise, consider one of many half- or full-day trips from downtown Stockholm to the archipelago. Hopping the local ferries to visit an island or two and see the lazy comings and goings of the island vacationers makes for a great day.

Shopping in Stockholm

Sweden offers a world of shopping temptations. **Nordiska Kompaniet** (NK, short for "no kronor left"), Stockholm's top-end department store, is located in an elegant early 20th-century building that dominates the far end of Kungsträdgården. If it feels like an old-time American department store, that's because its architect was inspired by grand stores he'd seen in the US (circa 1910). The Swedish design section (downstairs) and the kitchenware section are particularly impressive.

The classy **Gallerian** mall is just up the street from NK and stretches seductively nearly to Sergels Torg. The **Åhléns** store, nearby at Sergels Torg, is less expensive than NK and has two cafeterias and a supermarket. Fashion-forward **H&M** is right across the street. Drottninggatan is a long pedestrian boulevard lined with shops.

Designtorget, a store dedicated to contemporary Swedish design, receives a commission for selling the unique works of local designers (Mon-Fri 10:00-19:00, Sat 10:00-18:00, Sun 11:00-17:00, underneath Sergels Torg—enter from basement level of Kulturhuset, tel. 08/219-150, www.designtorget.se).

For more on Swedish design, pick up the *Design Guide* flier at the TI (listing smaller stores throughout town with a flair for design). The trendy and exclusive shops (including Orrefors and Kosta) line Biblioteksgatan just off Stureplan.

Traditionally, stores are open weekdays 10:00-18:00, Saturdays until 17:00, and Sundays 11:00-16:00. Some of the bigger stores (such as NK, H&M, and Åhléns) are open later on Saturdays and Sundays.

For a *smörgåsbord* of Scanjunk, visit the **Loppmarknaden,** northern Europe's biggest flea market, at the planned suburb of Skärholmen (free entry on weekdays, 15 kr on weekends—when it's busiest, Mon-Fri 11:00-18:00, Sat 10:00-16:00, Sun 11:00-16:00, T-bana: Varberg—on line #13—is just steps from the shopping action, tel. 08/710-0060, www.loppmarknaden.se). Hötorget, the produce market, also hosts a Sunday flea market in summer.

Stockholms Stadsmission's secondhand shop in Gamla Stan is a great place to pick up an unusual gift and contribute to this worthwhile charity (near Stortorget at Trångsund 8, Mon-Fri 10:00-18:00, Sat 11:00-16:00, closed Sun, tel. 08/787-8682, www.stadsmissionen.se/secondhand).

Systembolaget is Sweden's state-run liquor store chain. A sample of each bottle of wine or liquor sits in a display case. A card in front explains how it tastes and suggests menu pairings. Look for the item number and order at the counter. There's a branch on Gamla Stan at Lilla Nygatan 18, in Hörtorget underneath the movie theater complex, and in Norrmalm at Vasagatan 21 (Mon-Wed 10:00-18:00, Thu-Fri 10:00-19:00, Sat 10:00-15:00, closed Sun, www.systembolaget.se).

Nightlife in Stockholm

Bars and Music in Gamla Stan—The street called Stora Nygatan, with several lively bars, has perhaps the most accessible and reliable place for good jazz in town: Stampen.

Stampen Jazz & Rhythm n' Blues Pub has two venues: a stone-vaulted cellar below and a fun-loving saloon-like bar upstairs (check out the old instruments and antiques hanging from the ceiling). From Monday through Thursday, there's live music only in the saloon. On Friday and Saturday, bands alternate sets in both the saloon and the cellar (140-kr cover Fri-Sat only, 50-kr beers, open Mon-Sat 20:00-1:00 in the morning, even later Fri-Sat, free blues Mon-Thu, special free jam session Sat 14:00-18:00, closed Sun, Stora Nygatan 5, tel. 08/205-793, www.stampen.se).

Several other lively spots are within a couple of blocks of

Stampen on Stora Nygatan, including **Wirtströms Pub** (live blues bands play in crowded cellar Tue-Sat 21:00-24:00, no cover, 60-kr beers, open daily 12:00-1:00 in the morning, Stora Nygatan 13, www.wirstromspub.se) and **O'Connells Irish Pub** (a lively expat sports bar with music downstairs, daily 12:00-1:00 in the morning, Stora Nygatan 21, www.oconnells.se). Just beyond Gamla Stan, the good ship *Patricia* rocks with live music and well-lubricated locals most nights (no cover, often live music). Another pub with music is a few doors down.

Icebar Stockholm—If you just want to put on a heavy coat and gloves and drink a fancy vodka in a modern-day igloo, consider the fun, if touristy, Icebar Stockholm. Everything's ice— shipped down from Sweden's far north. The bar, the glasses, even the tip jar are made of ice. You get your choice of vodka drinks and 45 minutes to enjoy the scene (online booking-180 kr, drop-in after 21:45-195 kr, additional drinks-95 kr, reserva-tions smart; daily June-Aug 13:00-24:00, Sept-May 15:00-24:00; last entry 45 minutes before closing, in the Nordic Sea Hotel adjacent to the main train station at Vasaplan 4, tel. 08/5056-3124, www.icebar.se). People are let in all at once every 45 minutes. That means there's a long line for drinks, and the place goes from being very crowded to almost empty as people gradually melt away. At first everyone's just snapping photos. While there are ice bars all over Europe now, this is the second one (after the Ice Hotel in Lapland). And it really is pretty cool...a steady 23°F.

Cinema—In Sweden, international movies are shown in their original language with Swedish subtitles. Swedish theaters sometimes charge more for longer films (95-110 kr, movies longer than 2 hours are usually the higher price), and tickets come with assigned seats (drop by to choose seats and buy a ticket, box offices generally open 11:00-22:00 daily). The Hötorget and Drottninggatan neighborhoods have many theaters.

Sleeping in Stockholm

Peak season for Stockholm's hotels—weeknights outside of summer vacation time—is dictated by business travelers. Rates drop by 30-50 percent in the summer (mid-June-mid-Aug) and on Friday and Saturday nights year-round. Because many hotels set prices based on demand, rates listed in this section can have a wide range. If you ask for discounts and comparison-shop, you're likely to save

Sleep Code

(6 kr = about $1, country code: 46, area code: 08)
S = Single, **D** = Double/Twin, **T** = Triple, **Q** = Quad, **b** = bathroom, **s** = shower. Unless otherwise noted, all of my listings have non-smoking rooms and elevators, accept credit cards, and include big breakfast buffets. Everyone speaks English.

To help you sort easily through these listings, I've divided the accommodations into three categories, based on the price for a standard double room with bath during high season:

$$$ **Higher Priced**—Most rooms 1,700 kr or more.
  $$ **Moderately Priced**—Most rooms between 800-1,700 kr.
    $ **Lower Priced**—Most rooms 800 kr or less.

Prices can change without notice; verify the hotel's current rates online or by email. For other updates, see www .ricksteves.com/update.

plenty.

Plenty of people offer private accommodations (600-800-kr doubles). Stockholm's hostels are among Europe's best, offering good beds in simple but interesting places for about 300 kr per night. Each has helpful English-speaking staff, pleasant family rooms, and good facilities. Hosteling is cheapest when you're a member, provide your own sheets, and buy your own food for breakfast.

A program called **Destination Stockholm** is, for many (especially families), the best way to book a big hotel on weekends or during the summer. When you reserve a hotel room through this service, a **Stockholm à la Carte** card is thrown in for free. It covers public transportation, most major sights, and lots of tours—and is even better than the Stockholm Card. Kids sleep and get cards for free, too. The card is valid every day of your stay, including arrival and departure days. Reserve by phone or online; be sure to review the cancellation policy before you commit (tel. 08/663-0080, www .destination-stockholm.com).

In Downtown Norrmalm, near the Train Station

$$$ Freys Hotel is a Scan-mod, four-star place, with 124 compact, smartly designed rooms on a quiet pedestrian street. While big, it works hard to be friendly and welcoming. It's well-situated, located on a dead-end street across from the central train station. Its cool, candlelit breakfast room becomes a bar in the evening, popular for its selection of Belgian microbrews (Sb-1,050-1,750 kr,

STOCKHOLM

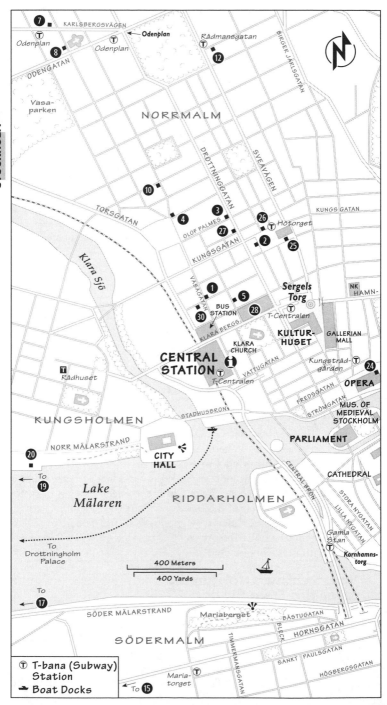

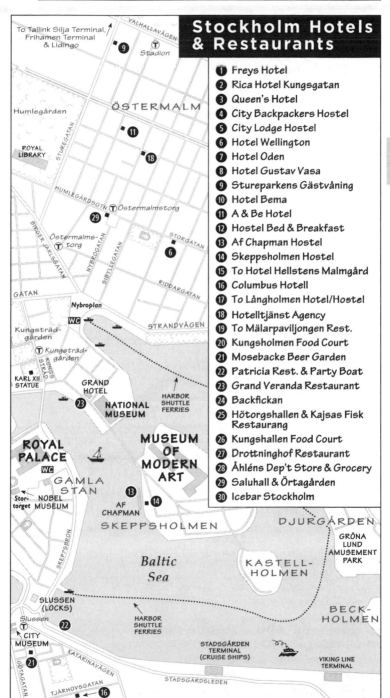

Stockholm Hotels & Restaurants

1. Freys Hotel
2. Rica Hotel Kungsgatan
3. Queen's Hotel
4. City Backpackers Hostel
5. City Lodge Hostel
6. Hotel Wellington
7. Hotel Oden
8. Hotel Gustav Vasa
9. Stureparkens Gästvåning
10. Hotel Bema
11. A & Be Hotel
12. Hostel Bed & Breakfast
13. Af Chapman Hostel
14. Skeppsholmen Hostel
15. To Hotel Hellstens Malmgård
16. Columbus Hotell
17. To Långholmen Hotel/Hostel
18. Hotelltjänst Agency
19. To Mälarpaviljongen Rest.
20. Kungsholmen Food Court
21. Mosebacke Beer Garden
22. Patricia Rest. & Party Boat
23. Grand Veranda Restaurant
24. Backfickan
25. Hötorgshallen & Kajsas Fisk Restaurang
26. Kungshallen Food Court
27. Drottninghof Restaurant
28. Åhléns Dep't Store & Grocery
29. Saluhall & Örtagården
30. Icebar Stockholm

Db-1,550-2,050 kr, Bryggargatan 12, Internet access, tel. 08/5062-1300, fax 08/5062-1313, www.freyshotels.com, freys@freyshotels.com). Check their website for summer specials.

$$ Rica Hotel Kungsgatan, central but characterless, fills the top floors of a downsized department store with 270 rooms. If the Starship *Enterprise* had a low-end hotel, this would be it. Save 150-400 kr by taking a room with no windows—the same size as other rooms, extremely quiet, and well-ventilated. This is the rare hotel where you'll get the best price by booking online with a travel website—calling direct will get you a more expensive rate (Db-1,200-1,700 kr, Kungsgatan 47, tel. 08/723-7220, fax 08/723-7299, www.rica.se).

$$ Queen's Hotel enjoys a great location at the quiet top end of Stockholm's main pedestrian shopping street (about a 10-minute walk from the train station or Gamla Stan). The 52 well-priced rooms feel old-fashioned but have been renovated, and the plush Old World lounge is inviting. Three types of double rooms vary only in size (Sb-1,020- 1,220 kr, "small standard" Db-1,120-1,320 kr, "large standard" Db-1,220-1,520 kr, "superior" Db with pull-out sofa bed-1,320-1,620 kr, 10 percent discount for readers who book direct—be sure to ask for it, extra bed-250 kr, elevator, free Internet access and Wi-Fi, Drottninggatan 71A, tel. 08/249-460, fax 08/217-620, www.queenshotel.se, info@queenshotel.se).

$ City Backpackers is central—a quarter-mile from the station—and open year-round. It's enthusiastically run, with 220 beds and plenty of creativity (bunk in 8-bed room-190 kr, bunk in 4- or 6-bed room-280 kr, bunk-bed D-650 kr, 40 percent more for Fri- or Sat-night stay without weeknight, sheets-50 kr, free cook-it-yourself pasta, breakfast-40 kr, laundry, free Internet access and Wi-Fi, movies, sauna, lockers, kitchen, shoes-off policy, Upplandsgatan 2A, tel. 08/206-920, fax 08/100-464, www.citybackpackers.se, info@citybackpackers.se).

$ City Lodge Hostel, new and well-run, is just a block in front of the central train station on a quiet side street. It has a convivial lounge, kitchen, free Internet access, laundry, and no curfew. It's a good value for backpackers in Stockholm (65 beds, bunk in 18-bed dorm-220 kr, in 6-bed dorm-270 kr, in quad-315 kr, a few tiny bunk-bed doubles-640 kr, cheaper outside of summer, sheets-50 kr, 60-kr breakfast available, Klara Norra Kyrkogata 15, tel. 08/226-630, www.citylodge.se, info@citylodge.se).

In Norrmalm and Östermalm, in Quieter Residential Areas

These options are in stately, elegant neighborhoods of five- and six-story turn-of-the-century apartment buildings. All are too far to walk from the station with luggage, but still in easy reach of downtown sights and close to T-bana stops.

$$$ Hotel Wellington, two blocks off Östermalmstorg square, is in a less handy but charming part of town. It's modern and bright, with hardwood floors, 60 rooms, and a friendly welcome. While expensive, this hotel offers great amenities and is a cut above in comfort (Sb-1,095-2,095 kr, Db-1,695-2,695 kr, smaller Db for 200 kr less, fill out their Choice Card and save 5 percent, mention this book when reserving and you might save a little more, free Internet access, sauna, old-fashioned English bar, free buffet in the evening helps your wallet and your waistline, T-bana: Östermalmstorg, exit to Storgatan and walk toward big church to Storgatan 6; tel. 08/667-0910, fax 08/667-1254, www .wellington.se, cc.wellington@choice.se).

$$ Hotel Oden, a recently renovated 140-room place with all the comforts, is three T-bana stops from the train station (Sb-925-1,365 kr, Db-1,195-1,695 kr, extra bed-145-170 kr, sauna, free Internet access and Wi-Fi, free coffee and tea in the evening; T-bana: Odenplan, exit in direction of Västmannagatan, Karlbergsvägen 24; tel. 08/457-9700, fax 08/457-9710, www.hotel oden.se). Some rooms come with a kitchenette for the same price (just request one).

$$ Hotel Gustav Vasa, a half-block from Hotel Oden (and not as good), rents 42 rooms on several floors of a late-19th-century apartment building (S-600-1,000 kr, Sb-1,000-1,250 kr, Db-1,690-1,950 kr, lower in summer if you book two months in advance, T-bana: Odenplan, Västmannagatan 61, tel. 08/343-801, fax 08/307-372, www.gustavvasahotel.se, info@gustavvasahotel .se).

$$ Stureparkens Gästvåning, carefully run by Challe, an Iraqi-Swede, is one floor of an apartment building converted into nine bright, clean, quiet, and thoughtfully appointed rooms. Only two rooms have private bathrooms (S-850 kr, D-895-990 kr, Tb-1,495 kr, sprawling Db apartment-1,950 kr, kitchen, guest laundry facility, free Internet access; T-bana: Stadion, across from Stureparken at Sturegatan 58, take elevator to fourth floor; tel. 08/662-7230, fax 08/661-5713, www.stureparkens.nu, info @stureparkens.nu).

$$ Hotel Bema is a humble place that rents out 12 fine rooms for some of the best prices in town (S-650-850 kr, Db-850-1,050 kr, extra person-250 kr, breakfast served in room, bus #65 from station to Upplandsgatan 13, tel. 08/232-675, www.hotelbema.se, hotell.bema@stockholm.mail.telia.com).

$$ A & Be Hotel, with 12 homey rooms, fills the first floor of a grand old building in a residential area (S-540 kr, Sb-840 kr, D-690 kr, Db-990 kr, breakfast-50 kr, free Wi-Fi, T-bana: Stadion, Grev Turegatan 50, tel. 08/660-2100, fax 08/660-5987, www.abehotel.com, info@abehotel.com).

$ Hostel Bed and Breakfast is a tiny, woody, and easygoing independent hostel renting 39 cheap beds in various dorm-style rooms. Many families stay here (bed in 4-bed room-290 kr, Sb-510 kr, Db-740 kr, sheets-50 kr, kitchen, laundry, across the street from T-bana: Rådmansgatan, just off Sveavägen at Rehnsgatan 21, tel. & fax 08/152-838, www.hostelbedandbreakfast .com).

On Gamla Stan and Skeppsholmen

These options are in the midst of sightseeing, a short bus or taxi ride from the train station.

$$$ Rica Hotel Gamla Stan offers Old World elegance in the heart of Gamla Stan (a 5-minute walk from Gamla Stan T-bana station). Its 51 small rooms are filled with chandeliers and hardwood floors (Sb-900- 1,800 kr, Db-1,200-2,200 kr, 200 kr extra for larger room, Lilla Nygatan 25, tel. 08/723-7250, fax 08/723-7259, www.rica.se, info.gamlastan@rica.se).

$$$ Lady Hamilton Hotel, expensive and lavishly furnished, is shoehorned into Gamla Stan on a quiet street a block below the cathedral and Royal Palace. The centuries-old building has 34 small, plush rooms and is filled with antiques and thoughtful touches (Db-1,450-3,200 kr, free Internet access, Storkyrkobrinken 5, tel. 08/5064-0100, fax 08/5064-0110, www.ladyhamiltonhotel .se, info@ladyhamiltonhotel.se).

$ Af Chapman Hostel, a permanently moored 100-year-old schooner, is Europe's most famous youth hostel and has provided a berth for the backpacking crowd for years. Renovated from keel to stern, the old salt offers 120 bunks in two- to six-bed rooms (310 kr, lockout daily 11:00-15:00). Reception and breakfast are at Skeppsholmen Hostel (next).

$ Skeppsholmen Hostel, just ashore from the *Af Chapman*, has 160 beds (bunk in 17-bed dorm-310 kr, D-690 kr, 50 kr less for hostel members, sheets-70 kr, breakfast-80 kr, laundry service, no lockout, bus #65 from train station or walk about 20 minutes, tel. 08/463-2266, www.stfchapman.com, chapman@stfturist.se).

On or near Södermalm

Södermalm is residential and hip, with Stockholm's best café and bar scene. You'll need to take the bus or T-bana to get here from the train station.

$$ Hotel Hellstens Malmgård is an eclectic collage of 52 rooms crammed with antiques in a circa-1770 mansion. No two rooms are alike, but all have modern baths and quirky touches such as porcelain stoves or four-poster beds. Unwind in its secluded cobblestone courtyard, and you may forget what century you're in

(Sb-690-1,290 kr, Db-890-1,490 kr, elevator, free Wi-Fi; T-bana: Zinkensdamm, then a 5-minute walk to Brännkyrkagatan 110; tel. 08/4650-5800, fax 08/661-8600, www.hellstensmalmgard.se, hotel@hellstensmalmgard.se).

$$ Columbus Hotell—located in a 19th-century building that formerly housed a brewery, a jail, and a hospital—has 69 quiet rooms in the heart of Södermalm. Half of its rooms (first and second floors) have private facilities. Third-floor rooms have facilities down the hall (S-845 kr, Sb-995-1,350 kr, D-995 kr, Db-1,350-1,650 kr, T-1,250 kr, no elevator; T-bana: Medborgarplatsen or bus #53 from train station to Tjärhovsplan, then a 5-minute walk to Tjärhovsgatan 11; tel. 08/5031-1200, fax 08/5031-1201, www .columbushotell.se, info@columbushotell.se).

$$ Långholmen Hotel/Hostel is on Långholmen, a small island off Södermalm that was transformed in the 1980s from Stockholm's main prison into a lovely park. Rooms are converted cells in the old prison building. You can choose between hostel- and hotel-standard rooms at many different price levels (hostel rooms: dorm bed-290 kr, D-690 kr, Tb-990 kr, Q-1,160 kr, 50-kr discount for hostel members, sheets-60 kr, breakfast-90 kr; hotel rooms: Db-1,700-1,890 kr, extra bed-250 kr, includes breakfast; free Wi-Fi, laundry room, kitchen, cafeteria, free parking, on-site swimming; T-bana: Hornstull, walk 10 minutes down and cross small bridge to Långholmen island, follow hotel signs 5 minutes farther; tel. 08/720-8500, fax 08/720-8575, www.langholmen.com, hotel@langholmen.com).

Rooms in Private Homes

Stockholm's private rooms can be a deal in high season if you want to have an at-home experience. During hotels' weekend/summer discount periods, private rooms don't save you much over a hotel. Be sure to get the front-door security code when you call, in case there's no intercom. Contact **Hotelltjänst,** a private-room booking agency (S-600 kr, D-750 kr, cash only, no breakfast, 2-night minimum; fully furnished apartments also available: Sb-800 kr, Db-1,200 kr; rates vary based on demand, Nybrogatan 44, tel. 08/104-437, fax 08/213-716, www.hotelltjanst.com, caretaker @hotelltjanst.com).

Eating in Stockholm

To save money, eat your main meal at lunch, when cafés and restaurants have 95-kr daily special plates called *dagens rätt* (generally Mon-Fri only). Most museums have handy cafés (with lots of turnover and therefore fresh food, 100-kr lunch deals, and often with fine views). Convenience stores serve gas station-style food (and often have seats). As anywhere, department stores and malls are eager to feed shoppers and can be a good, efficient choice. If you want culturally appropriate fast food, stop by a local hot dog stand. Picnics are a great option—especially for dinner, when restaurant prices are highest. There are plenty of park-like, harborside spots to give your cheap picnic some class.

In Gamla Stan

Most restaurants in Gamla Stan serve the 95-kr weekday lunch special mentioned above, which comes with a main dish, small salad,

bread, and free tap water. Choose from Swedish, Asian, or Italian cuisine. Several popular places are right on the main square (Stortorget) and near the cathedral. Järntorget, at the far end, is another fun tables-in-the-square scene and has a small Co-op Nara supermarket for picnic shopping. The Munkbrohallen supermarket downstairs in the Gamla Stan T-bana station is very picnic-friendly (daily 7:00-22:00). Touristy places line Västerlånggatan. You'll find more romantic spots hiding on side lanes. I've listed my favorites below (for locations, see the map on opposite page).

Grillska Huset is a cheap and handy cafeteria run by Stockholms Stadsmission, a charitable organization helping the poor. It's grandly situated right on the old square, with indoor and outdoor seating (tranquil garden up the stairs and out back), fine daily specials, a hearty salad bar, and a staff committed to helping others. You can feed the hungry (that's you) and help house the homeless at the same time. The 85-kr daily special gets you a hot plate, salad, and coffee, or choose the 85-kr salad bar—both available Mon-Fri 11:00-14:00 (café serves sandwiches and salads daily 9:00-18:00, Stortorget 3, tel. 08/787-8605). They also have a fine little bakery.

Vapiano Pasta Pizza Bar, a mod, high-energy Italian place, issues you an electronic card as you enter. Circulate, ordering up whatever you like as they swipe your card. It's fun to oversee the construction of your 100-kr pasta, pizza, or salad. Portions are huge and easily splittable. As you leave, your card indicates the bill. Season things by picking a leaf of basil or rosemary from the potted plant on your table. Because tables are often shared, this a great place for solo travelers. They have Pilsner Urquell on tap but watch out—my glass of Chianti cost more than my pizza (daily 11:00-24:00, Fri-Sat until 1:00 in the morning, right next to entrance to

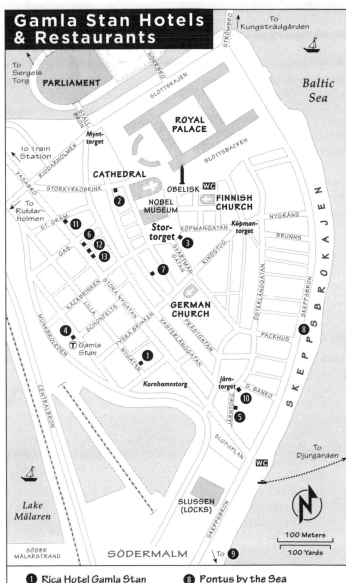

Gamla Stan Hotels & Restaurants

To Kungsträdgården

To Sergels Torg

PARLIAMENT

ROYAL PALACE

Baltic Sea

To Train Station

Mynt-torget

CATHEDRAL

To Riddar-holmen

OBELISK

WC

FINNISH CHURCH

NOBEL MUSEUM

Stor-torget

Köpman-torget

GERMAN CHURCH

Gamla Stan

Kornhamnstorg

Järn-torget

To Djurgården

Lake Mälaren

WC

SLUSSEN (LOCKS)

100 Meters

100 Yards

SÖDER MÄLARSTRAND

SÖDERMALM

To ⑨

SKEPPSBROKAJEN

- ① Rica Hotel Gamla Stan
- ② Lady Hamilton Hotel
- ③ Grillska Huset Cafeteria
- ④ Vapiano Pasta Pizza Bar
- ⑤ O'Leary's Sports Bar
- ⑥ Hermitage Restaurant
- ⑦ Kryp In Restaurant
- ⑧ Pontus by the Sea
- ⑨ To Mosebacke Beer Garden; Patricia Rest. & Party Boat
- ⑩ Co-op Nara Supermarket
- ⑪ Stampen Jazz & R-n-B Pub
- ⑫ Wirtströms Pub
- ⑬ O'Connells Irish Pub

Gamla Stan T-bana station, Munkbrogatan 8, tel. 08/222-940).

O'Leary's Sports Bar is a smoky place that transports you to Ireland. While sloppy, it's good for basic pub grub and beer. And if a game is on, this is the place to be—their motto is, "Better than live" (120-kr meals, Järntorgsgatan 3, tel. 08/239-923).

Hermitage Restaurant serves tasty vegetarian food in a warm communal dining setting. Their daily special (100-kr lunch, 110-kr dinner after 15:00) buys a hot plate, salad, bread, and coffee (Mon-Fri 11:00-20:00, Sat-Sun 12:00-20:00, Stora Nygatan 11, tel. 08/411-9500).

Kryp In, a small, cozy restaurant (the name means "hide away") tucked into a peaceful lane, has a stylish hardwood and candlelit interior, great sidewalk seating, and an open kitchen letting you in on Vladimir's artistry. If you dine well in Stockholm once (or twice), I'd do it here. It's gourmet without pretense. They serve delicious, modern Swedish cuisine with a 445-kr three-course dinner. From June to August, they have weekend lunch specials starting at 120 kr. Reserve ahead for dinner (200-250-kr plates, Mon-Fri 17:00-23:00, Sat 12:30-23:00, open Sun only in summer 12:30-22:00, a block off Stortorget at Prästgatan 17, tel. 08/208-841).

Harborview Dining in Gamla Stan and Östermalm

Pontus by the Sea is a classy restaurant with a long, covered, and heated veranda offering grand harbor views. Pontus is well-respected for its modern mix of French and Swedish cuisine. Half the place is a sofas-on-the-harbor cocktail lounge. Though the restaurant is pricey, their bar menu offers some deals. Call to reserve a harborside table (daily 12:00-24:00, off-season closed Sun, Tullhus 2, tel. 08/202-095).

Djurgårdsbrons Sjöcafe, beautifully situated and greedily soaking up the afternoon sun, fills a woody terrace stretching along the harbor just over the Djurgårdsbron bridge. In summer, this is a fine place for a meal or just a drink before or after your Skansen or *Vasa* visit. They have cheap lunch plates (90 kr, Mon-Fri 11:00-13:00 only); at other times, you'll pay 130-180 kr per plate (order at the bar, daily 11:00-22:00, closed off-season, behind the bike-rental hut, tel. 08/661-4488).

Dinner Cruises: The Palace Park Dinner Cruise sails nightly from Stadshusbron, offering a three-course dinner during a scenic cruise that includes a walking tour of the gardens at Drottningholm Palace (565 kr, drinks extra, three-hour cruise, departs daily in summer 17:30-22:00, tel. 08/1200-4000, www.stromma.se).

Fika: Sweden's Coffee Break

Swedes drink more coffee per capita than just about any other country in the world. The Swedish coffee break—or *fika*—is a ritual. *Fika* is to Sweden what teatime is to Britain. The typical *fika* is a morning or afternoon break in the workday, but can happen any time, any day. It's the perfect opportunity (and excuse) for tourists to take a break as well.

Fika-fare is coffee with a snack—something sweet or savory. Your best bet is a *kanelbulle,* a Swedish cinnamon bun, although some prefer *pariserbulle,* a bun filled with vanilla cream. These can be found nearly everywhere coffee is sold, including just about any café or *konditori* (bakery) in Stockholm. A coffee and a cinnamon bun in a café will cost you about 40 kr. (Most cafés will give you a coffee refill for free.) But at Pressbyrån, the Swedish convenience stores found all over town, you can satisfy your *fika*-fix for 25 kr by getting a coffee and bun to go. Grab a park bench or waterside perch, relax, and enjoy.

In Kungsholmen: Lakefront Behind City Hall

On a balmy summer's eve, **Mälarpaviljongen** is a dreamy spot with hundreds of locals enjoying the perfect lakefront scene, as trendy glasses of rosé shine like convivial lanterns. From City Hall, walk 15 minutes along Lake Mälaren (a treat in itself) and you'll find a hundred casual outdoor tables on a floating restaurant and among the trees on shore. Line up at the cafeteria to order a drink, snack, or complete meal. If it's cool, they have heaters and blankets. The walk along the lake back into town caps the experience beautifully (56-kr beer, 125-kr cocktails, 100-kr lunch plates, 150-200-kr evening plates, open in good weather April-Sept daily 11:00-late, easy lakeside walk or T-bana to Freedomsplace plus a 5-minute walk to Nörr Mälarstrand 63, no reservations, tel. 08/650-8701).

Kungsholmen is a high-energy food court surrounded by six open "bars," with busy kitchens serving six different cuisines from Asian to fish. This is a trendy scene. It's a bit pricey, but with big portions, reliable quality, no tourists, and a classy local clientele (200-300-kr plates; May-Sept daily 17:00-1:00 in the morning; Oct-April Tue-Sat 17:00-1:00 in the morning, closed Sun-Mon; from City Hall walk along Lake Mälaren five minutes to Nörr Mälarstrand Kajplats 464, tel. 08/5052-4450, www.kungsholmen .com).

STOCKHOLM

In Södermalm: Noisy Locals and Lots of Beer

Mosebacke is a gravelly beer garden with a grand harbor view, perched high above town just past Slussen in Södermalm. Open only on warm summer evenings and priding itself on its beer rather than the cheap grub, it's a good place to mix with a relaxed young crowd (a block inland from the top of the Katarina viewing platform, occasional live music, Mosebacke Torg 3, tel. 08/556-09890).

Patricia **Restaurant and Party Boat** is a fun, raucous place to enjoy a basic Swedish meal surrounded by good-time Swedes. The menu on this old steamer is a fun-loving surf-and-turf mix, with 250-kr plates and a 139-kr lobster feed on Wednesday nights. The boat has one deck packed with dinner tables, a bar on the top deck, and two dance zones below: one that's a *schlager* pop bar and dance floor, and the other that's a late-night disco. The boat really rocks with live music on weekends (music from 20:00, cover charge after 22:00). Consider having dinner here beforehand to get in free (Wed-Thu from 17:00, Fri-Sun from 18:00 until late, gay night on Sun, closed Mon-Tue, 200 yards past Djurgården boat dock, near Slussen at Stadsgårdskajen 152, tel. 08/743-0570, www.patricia.st).

On Norrmalm

Royal *Smörgåsbord* at the Grand Hotel

To stuff yourself with all the traditional Swedish specialties (a dozen kinds of herring, salmon, reindeer, meatballs, lingonberries, and shrimp, followed by a fine table of cheeses and desserts) with a super harbor view, consider splurging at the Grand Hotel's dressy **Grand Veranda Restaurant.** While very touristy and a bit tired, this is the finest *smörgåsbord* in town. The Grand Hotel, where royal guests and Nobel Prize winners stay, faces the harbor across from the palace. Pick up their English flier for a good explanation of the proper way to enjoy this grand buffet. Reservations are necessary (475 kr, tap water is free, other drinks extra, nightly 18:00-22:00, Sat-Sun also 13:00-16:00, May-Sept also Mon-Fri 12:00-15:00, no shorts, Södra Blasieholmshamnen 8, tel. 08/679-3586).

At the Royal Opera House

The Operakällaren, one of Stockholm's most exclusive restaurants, runs a little "hip pocket" restaurant called **Backfickan** on the side, specializing in traditional Swedish quality cooking at reasonable prices. It's ideal for someone eating out alone, or for anyone wanting an early dinner (they serve daily specials from 12:00 all the way up to 20:00). Sit inside—at tiny private side tables or at the big counter with the locals—or, in good weather, grab a table on the sidewalk. Choose from two different daily specials (about 150-200 kr), or pay 200-250 kr for main dishes from their regular menu (Mon-Sat 12:00-22:00, closed Sun, on the inland side of Royal Opera House, tel. 08/676-5809).

At or near Hötorget

Hötorget ("Hay Market"), a vibrant outdoor produce market just two blocks from Sergels Torg, is a fun place to picnic-shop. The outdoor market closes at 18:00, and many merchants put their unsold produce on the push list (earlier closing and more desperate merchants on Sat).

Hötorgshallen, next to Hötorget (in the basement under the modern cinema complex), is a colorful indoor food market with an old-fashioned bustle, plenty of exotic and ethnic edibles, and—in the tradition of food markets all over Europe—some great little eateries. The best is **Kajsas Fisk Restaurang,** hiding behind the fish stalls. They serve delicious fish soup to little Olivers who can hardly believe they're getting...more. For 85 kr, you get a big bowl of hearty soup, a simple salad, bread and crackers, butter, and water—plus one soup refill (100-kr daily fish specials, Mon-Fri 11:00-18:00, Sat 11:00-16:00, closed Sun, Hötorgshallen 3, tel. 08/207-262).

Kungshallen, an 800-seat indoor food court across the street from Hötorget, has 14 eateries—mostly chain restaurants and fast-food counters, including Chinese, sushi, pizza, Greek, and Mexican (Mon-Fri 9:00-23:00, Sat-Sun 12:00-23:00).

Drottninghof is a busy place with tables perfectly positioned for people-watching on the busy pedestrian boulevard (good-value 159-kr dinner specials, hearty 150-250-kr plates, Mon-Thu 11:00-24:00, Fri-Sat 11:00-1:00 in the morning, Sun 12:00-23:00, Drottninggatan 67, tel. 08/227 522).

Near Sergels Torg

The many modern shopping malls and department stores around Sergels Torg all have appealing, if pricey, eateries catering to the needs of hungry local shoppers. **Åhléns** department store has a Hemköp supermarket in the basement (Mon-Fri 8:00-21:00, Sat-Sun 10:00-21:00) and two restaurants upstairs with 80-110-kr daily lunch specials (Mon-Fri 11:00-19:30, Sat 11:00-18:30, Sun 11:00-17:30).

In Östermalm

Saluhall, on Östermalmstorg square (near recommended Hotel Wellington), is a great old-time indoor market with

plenty of fun eateries (Mon-Thu 9:30-18:00, Fri until 17:30, Sat until 16:00, closed Sun). Upstairs, the **Örtagården,** primarily a vegetarian restaurant, serves a 99-kr buffet weekdays until 17:00 and a larger 129-kr buffet evenings and weekends (Mon-Fri 10:30-22:00, Sat-Sun 11:00-21:00, entrance on side of market building at Nybrogatan 31, tel. 08/662-1728).

Stockholm Connections

By Bus

Unless you have a railpass, long-distance buses are cheaper than trains, such as from Stockholm to Oslo or Kalmar. Buses usually take longer, but have more predictable pricing, shorter ticket lines, and student discounts. Swebus is the largest operator (tel. 0771-21-8218, www.swebus.se); Säfflebussen also has lots of routes, including to Oslo (www.safflebussen.se). It's worth knowing about discount offers: Buy tickets at least 24 hours ahead for Swebus discounts; Säfflebussen cuts ticket prices on low-demand days and times.

From Stockholm by Bus to: Copenhagen (2/day, 9 hours), **Oslo** (3/day, 8 hours), **Kalmar** (4/day, fewer on weekends, 6 hours).

By Train

The easiest and cheapest way to book train tickets is online at www.sj.se. Simply select your journey and pay for it with a credit card. When you arrive at the train station, print out your tickets at a self-service ticket kiosk (bring your purchase confirmation code). You can also buy tickets at a ticket window in a train station, but this comes with long lines and a 5 percent surcharge. For timetables and prices, check online, call 0771/757-575, or use one of the self-service ticket kiosks.

As with airline tickets and hotel rooms, Swedish train ticket prices vary with demand. For intercity and regional trains, ask for the *"Just nu"* ("Just now") fare, which can earn you up to a 60 percent discount if you book far enough in advance.

For railpass-holders, seat reservations are required on express (X2000) and overnight trains, and recommended on some other trains (to Oslo, for example). Second-class seat reservations to Copenhagen cost 65 kr (150 kr in first class). If you have a railpass, make your seat reservation at a ticket window in a train station or by phone (not online or at self-service ticket kiosks).

From Stockholm by Train to: Uppsala (1-3/hour, 40 minutes), **Växjö** (every 2 hours, 3.5 hours, change in Alvesta, reservations required), **Kalmar** (12/day, 4.5-5 hours, transfer in Alvesta, reservations required), **Copenhagen** (almost hourly, 5-6 hours on high-speed train, some with a transfer at Lund or Hässleholm, reservation required; overnight train requires a change in Malmö or Lund; all trains stop at Copenhagen airport before terminating at the central station), **Oslo** (2/day direct Intercity trains, 6 hours; 2/day with change in Kristinehamn, 6 hours; plus a direct 9-hour night train in summer only).

By Boat

The boat companies run shuttle buses from the train station to coincide with each departure; check for details when you buy your ticket. When comparing prices between boats and planes, remember that the boat fare includes a night's lodging.

From Stockholm to: Helsinki and **Tallinn** (daily/nightly boats, 16 hours), **Turku** (daily/nightly boats, 11 hours).

By Plane

For information on arriving at Stockholm's airports, see "Arrival in Stockholm," earlier in this chapter.

To Helsinki and Tallinn: Many low-fare airlines are offering flights across the Baltic. For flights from Stockholm to Helsinki, check www.blue1.com; to Tallinn, also visit www.norwegian.com and www.estonian-air.com.

Route Tips for Drivers

Stockholm to Oslo: It's an eight-hour drive from Stockholm to Oslo. **Årjäng,** just before the Norwegian border, is a good place for a rest stop. At the border, change money at the little TI kiosk (on right side). Pick up the Oslo map and *What's On in Oslo,* and consider buying your Oslo Card here.

Near Stockholm: Uppsala

Uppsala is a compact city with a cathedral and university that win Sweden's "oldest/largest/tallest" awards. If you're not traveling anywhere else in Sweden other than Stockholm, Uppsala makes a pleasant day trip. But if you're short on time, Uppsala is not worth sacrificing time in Stockholm or a boat trip through the archipelago. If you visit, allow the better part of a day, including the trip out and back. During summer vacations, this university town is very quiet.

Getting There: Take the train from Stockholm's Central

STOCKHOLM

Station (1-3/hour, 40 minutes, 80 kr, buy tickets at ticket windows).
Since the Uppsala station has lockers and is in the same direction
from Stockholm as the airport, you could combine a quick visit
here with an early arrival or late departure.

Orientation to Uppsala

(area code: 018)

Tourist Information

The helpful TI, overlooking the canal through the heart of town,
has free maps and the informative *What's On Uppsala* magazine
(Mon-Fri 10:00-18:00, Sat 10:00-15:00, closed Sun except mid-
June-Aug open Sun 11:00-15:00, Fyristorg 8, tel. 018/727-4800,
www.uppsala.to).

Arrival in Uppsala

From the train station (lockers-20-30 kr), walk straight out the front
door, cross the busy street, and walk two blocks. Turn right along
the newly pedestrianized shopping street called Kungsängsgatan.

Walk three more blocks (passing the Åhléns department store, with its handy Hemköp grocery downstairs) and you'll run into the town's main square, Stora Torget. From here, you can turn left and cross the canal. The TI is just to the right after the canal, and you can see the cathedral spires (which also mark the university zone) just behind it.

Sights in Uppsala

▲▲Uppsala Cathedral (Domkyrkan)

One of Scandinavia's largest, most historic cathedrals feels as vital as it does impressive. The building was completed in 1453; the spires and interior decorations are from the late 19th century.

The cathedral—with a fine Gothic interior, the relics of St. Erik, and the tomb of King Gustav Vasa—is well worth a visit.

Cost and Hours: Free, open daily 8:00-18:00, tel. 018/187-177, www.uppsaladomkyrka.se.

Tours: Ask inside about **guided tours** in English (mid-June-mid-Aug Mon-Sat at 11:00 and 14:00, Sun at 16:00; off-season call to arrange). Or, just inside the nave, look for the self-service kiosk and buy the handy 10-kr **leaflet** outlining an excellent self-guided tour.

Touring the Cathedral: Near the entrance is the tomb and memorial to scientist Carolus Linnaeus, who created the formal system for naming different species of plants and animals. Farther

into the church you'll find the gorgeously carved, gold-slathered Baroque pulpit, and the transept where today's services take place. Look high above in the choir area (beyond the transept) to enjoy fine murals that gleam, thanks to a major restoration of the church in the 1970s.

At the far end of the church, don't disturb the woman peering toward the grave in the apse. This eerily lifelike statue from 2005, called *Mary (The Return),* captures Jesus' mother later in life, wearing a scarf and timeless garb. The chapel she's looking at once housed a shrine to her, but for more than 300 years after the Reformation, images of Mary were downplayed in this church. In keeping with the Protestant spirit here,

this new version of Mary is shown not as an exalted queen, but as an everywoman, saddened by the loss of her child and seeking solace—or answers—in the church.

Follow Mary's gaze into the chapel housing the **tomb of King Gustav Vasa** and his family. Notice that in the sculpture, Gustav is shown flanked by not one, but two wives—his first wife died after suffering a fall; his second wife bore him 10 children. The chapel is ringed with murals of his illustrious life.

Back at the entrance to the church, by the gift shop, you can pay to enter the **treasury** collection. Here you'll find medieval textiles (tapestries and vestments), swords and crowns found in Gustav's grave, and the Nobel Peace Prize won by Nathan Söderblom, an early-20th-century archbishop here (30 kr, Mon-Sat 10:00-17:00, Sun 12:30-17:00). In this same narthex area, notice the debit-card machine soliciting donations: The church doing its same old work in a new way.

University Attractions and Nearby Sights

Scandinavia's first university was founded here in 1477. Two famous grads are Carolus Linnaeus (father of modern taxonomy) and astronomer Anders Celsius (who developed the temperature scale that bears his name). The following two university buildings are interesting and open to non-students.

▲▲**Gustavianum**—Directly across from the cathedral is the university's oldest surviving building, with a bulbous dome that doubles as a sundial (notice the gold numbers). Today it houses

a well-presented museum that features an anatomical theater, a cabinet filled with miniature curiosities, and Celsius' thermometer. The collection is unaccountably engaging for the glimpse it gives into the mind-set of 17th-century Europe.

Cost and Hours: 50 kr, June-Aug Tue-Sun 10:00-16:00, Sept-May Tue-Sun 11:00-16:00, closed Mon year-round, tours in English Sat-Sun at 13:00, Akademigatan 3, tel. 018/471-7571, www.gustavianum.uu.se.

Touring the Gustavianum: Find the elevator (hiding near the gift shop/ticket desk) and ride it up to the fourth floor, then see the exhibits as you walk back down. Up top is a collection of artifacts discovered at Valsgärde, a prehistoric site near Uppsala used for burials for more than 700 years. Archaeologists have uncovered 15 boat graves here (dating from A.D. 600-1050—roughly one per generation), providing more insight on the Viking Age.

Next you'll find the museum's highlight, the anatomical theater (accessible from the fourth and third floors). Its only show was human dissection. In the mid-1600s, as the enlightened ideas of the Renaissance swept far into the north of Europe, scholars began to consider dissection of the human body the ultimate scientific education. Corpses of hanged criminals were carefully sliced and diced here, under a dome in an almost temple-like atmosphere, demonstrating the lofty heights to which science had risen in society. Imagine 200 students (and others who'd paid admission) standing tall all around and leaning in to peer intently at the teacher's scalpel.

Another floor down (on the second floor) is an exhibit on the history of the university, which is far more interesting than it sounds. The Physics Chamber features a collection of instruments from the 18th and 19th centuries that were used by university teachers. But the most fascinating item is in the room across the hall: the Augsburg Art Cabinet, a dizzying array of nearly a thousand miniscule works of art and other tidbits held in an ornately decorated oak cabinet. Built in the 1620s for a bigwig who wanted to impress his friends, the cabinet's contents are shown in display cases all around. Find the interactive video screen, where you can control a virtual tour of the collection. Beyond the cabinet and to the right is a thermometer once belonging to Celsius.

Rounding out the collection (on the first floor) is the university's collection from the Mediterranean: ancient Greek and Roman artifacts and Egyptian sarcophagi.

▲**University Library (Universitetsbiblioteket)**—Uppsala University's library, housed in a 19th-century building called the Carolina Rediviva, is just up the hill from the cathedral and Gustavianum. Off the entry hall (to the right) is a small exhibit of treasured old books. Well-displayed and well-described in English, the carefully selected collection is surprisingly captivating. The centerpiece of the exhibit, in its own room, is the sixth-century Silver Bible. Sweden's single most precious book is so named for its silver-ink writing (on purple-colored parchment) in the extinct Gothic language. You'll also see the Carta Marina, the first more-or-less accurate map of Scandinavia, created in 1539. Compare this 16th-century understanding of the region with your own travels.

Cost and Hours: 20 kr, free Oct-May; open Mon-Fri 9:00-20:00, Sat 10:00-17:00, closed Sun, tel. 018/471-3918, www.ub .uu.se.

More Sights near the University—The **Uppland Museum** (Upplandsmuseet), a regional history museum with prehistoric bits and folk-art scraps, is on the river by the waterfall, near the TI (free, Tue-Sun 12:00-17:00, closed Mon, tel. 018/169-100, www.upplandsmuseet.se). Uphill from the university library are the **botanical gardens** and a museum named after Linnaeus, and the 16th-century **Uppsala Castle,** which houses an art museum and runs slice-of-castle-life tours (required 80-kr tour, offered in English only a few weeks each summer Tue-Sun at 13:00 and 15:00, tel. 018/727-2485).

▲Gamla Uppsala

This site on the outskirts of town, which gives historians goose bumps even on a sunny day, includes nine large royal burial mounds circled by a walking path with English descriptions. Fifteen hundred years ago, when the Baltic Sea was higher and it was easy to sail all the way to Uppsala, the pagan Swedish kings had their capital here.

You can simply wander the grounds, or learn more by visiting the attractive Gamla Uppsala Museum, which gives a good overview of early Swedish history and displays items found in the mounds.

Cost and Hours: Grounds—free; museum—60 kr; May-Aug daily 10:00-16:00; Sept-Nov and Jan-April Mon, Wed, and Sat-Sun 12:00-15:00, closed Tue and Fri; closed Dec; included guided tours in English available May-Aug daily at 15:30, tel. 018/239-300, www.raa.se/gamlauppsala.

Nearby: The venerable **Gamla Uppsala church** dates from the 12th century (free, daily April-Aug 9:00-18:00, Sept-March 9:00-16:00).

Eating at Gamla Uppsala: Gamla Uppsala is great for picnics, or you can recharge at the half-timbered **Odinsborg café,** which serves sandwiches, mead, and buffets—including *smörgåsbord* in summer (café daily 10:00-18:00, restaurant daily 12:00-18:00—reservations required, tel. 018/323-525).

Getting There: From downtown Uppsala, go to the bus stop at Vaksalagatan 7-13 (a block and a half from Stora Torget, the main square) and take bus #2, marked *Gamla Uppsala*, to the last stop (30 kr, buy ticket at nearby Pressbyrån kiosk, 2-4/hour, 15-minute trip). Allow two or three hours for your visit, including the time it takes to bus there and back.

Eating in Uppsala

Eateries abound along the river and in the business district. **Dom-trappkällaren,** tucked behind the cathedral, serves up traditional Swedish meals in its characteristic interior or outside at streetside tables (110-kr lunches served Mon-Fri 11:00-14:30, then pricier dinners—100-210-kr starters, 185-325-kr main dishes; open Mon-Fri 11:00-23:00, Sat 17:00-23:00, closed Sun, St. Eriks Gränd, go through the little tunnel behind the cathedral and look left, tel. 018/130-955).

For picnic fixings, stop by **Hemköp,** a grocery located on the ground floor of Åhléns department store (Mon-Fri 7:00-22:00, Sat-Sun 9:00-22:00, on Stora Torget). Enjoy the picnic at one of Uppsala's parks, or join the locals down on the boardwalk along the river, below St. Olof's bridge.

STOCKHOLM

STOCKHOLM'S ARCHIPELAGO

Skärgården

Some of Europe's most scenic islands stretch from Stockholm 80 miles out into the Baltic Sea. If you're cruising to (or from) Finland, you'll get a good look at this island beauty. If you have more time and want to immerse yourself in all that simple Swedish nature, consider spending a day or two island-hopping.

The Swedish word for "island" is simply *ö*, but the local name for this area is *Skärgården*—literally "garden of skerries," unforested rocks sticking up from the sea. That stone is granite, carved out and deposited by glaciers. The archipelago closer to Stockholm is rockier, with bigger islands and more trees. Farther out (such as at Sandhamn), the glaciers lingered longer, slowly grinding the granite into sand and creating smaller islands.

Locals claim there are more than 30,000 of these islands, and as land here is rising slowly, more pop out every year. Some 150 are inhabited year-round, and about 100 have ferry service. There's an unwritten law of public access in the archipelago. Technically you're allowed to pitch your tent anywhere for up to two nights, provided the owner of the property can't see you from his or her house. It's polite to ask first and essential to act responsibly.

With thousands of islands to choose from, every Swede seems to have a favorite. This chapter covers four very different island destinations that offer an overview of the archipelago. Vaxholm, the gateway to the archipelago, comes with an imposing fortress, a charming fishermen's harbor, and the easiest connections to Stockholm. Rustic Grinda feels like—and used to be—a Swedish summer camp. Sparsely populated Svartsö is another fine back-to-nature experience. And swanky Sandhamn thrills the sailboat set, with a lively yacht harbor, a scenic setting at the far edge of the archipelago, and (true to its name) sandy beaches.

The flat-out best way to experience the magic of the archipelago is simply stretching out comfortably on the rooftop deck of your ferry. The journey truly is the destination. Enjoy the charm of lovingly painted cottages as you glide by, delicate pairs of lounge chairs positioned to catch just the right view and sun, the steady rhythm of the ferries lacing this world together, and people savoring quality time with each other and nature.

Planning Your Time

On a Tour: For the best quick look, consider one of the many half- or full-day package boat trips from downtown Stockholm to the archipelago. **Strömma Kanalbolaget** runs several options, including the three-hour Archipelago Tour (2-4/day, 220 kr), or the all-day Thousand Island Cruise (departs daily in summer at 9:30, 1,160 kr includes lunch and dinner). Or, to be efficient, combine a three-hour island joyride with a meal—choose between a lunch, brunch, or dinner cruise (tel. 08/1200-4000, www.stromma kanalbolaget.com).

On Your Own: For more flexibility, freedom, and a better dose of the local vacation scene, do it on your own. Any one of the islands in this chapter is easily doable as a single-day side-trip from Stockholm. And, because all boats to and from Stockholm pass through Vaxholm, it's easy to tack on that town to any other one.

For a very busy all-day itinerary that takes in the two most enjoyable island destinations (Grinda and Sandhamn), consider this plan: 8:00-Set sail from Stockholm; 9:30-Arrive in Grinda for a quick walk around the island; 10:50-Catch the boat to Sandhamn; 11:45-Arrive in Sandhamn, have lunch, and enjoy the town; 17:00-Catch boat to Stockholm (maybe have dinner on board); 19:05-Arrive back in Stockholm. Depending on your interests, you could craft a more in-depth route: For example, for a back-to-nature experience, try Stockholm-Grinda-Svartsö-Stockholm. For an urban mix of towns, consider Stockholm-Vaxholm-Sandhamn-Stockholm.

Overnighting on an island really lets you get away from it all and enjoy the island ambience. I've listed a few island accommodations, but note that mid-range options are few; most tend to be either pricey top-end or very rustic (rented cottages with minimal plumbing). Decide up front whether you want to splurge or rough it.

Don't struggle too hard with the "which island?" decision. The main thing is to get well beyond Vaxholm, where the scenery gets more striking. I'd sail an hour or two past Vaxholm, have a short stop on an island, then stop in Vaxholm on the way home. Again, the real joy is the view from your ferry.

Getting Around the Archipelago

A few archipelago destinations (including Vaxholm) are accessible overland, thanks to modern bridges. For other islands, you'll take a boat. Two major companies run public ferries from downtown Stockholm to the archipelago: the bigger Waxholmsbolaget and the smaller Cinderella Båtarna.

Tickets: Regular tickets are sold on board. Simply walk on, and at your convenience, stop by the desk to buy your ticket before you disembark. Waxholmsbolaget offers a deal that's worthwhile if you're traveling with a small group or doing a lot of island-hopping. You can save 25 percent by buying a 1,000-kr ticket credit for 750 kr (sold only on land; use the splittable credit to buy tickets on the boat). If you're staying in the archipelago for a few days and want to island-hop, consider the Boat Hiking Card. This five-day all-inclusive pass is good on either boat line (420 kr, plus a 40-kr refundable deposit). Buy the card at the Waxholmsbolaget office or at the Strandvägen information office listed below.

Schedules: Check both companies' schedules when planning your itinerary; you might have to mix and match to make your itinerary work. A single, confusing schedule booklet mixes together times for both lines. Ferry schedules are complex even to locals, especially outside of peak season.

It's essential to carefully review and confirm your plans, ideally at the information desk in the glassy house on the Strandvägen embankment. Attendants will help you sort through your options and plan your archipelago visit (May-Sept Mon-Fri 9:00-17:30, Sat-Sun 10:00-16:00; off-season Mon-Fri 10:00-16:00, closed Sat-Sun; Strandvägen Kajplats 18—that's boat landing #18, www.visits kargarden.se).

Note that the departures mentioned below are for summer (mid-June–mid-Aug); the number of boats declines off-season.

Waxholmsbolaget: Their ships depart across from Stockholm's Grand Hotel, at the stop called Stromkäjen (tel. 08/679-5830, www.waxholmsbolaget.se). Waxholmsbolaget boats run from Stockholm to: **Vaxholm** (at least hourly, 75 minutes, 75 kr), **Grinda** (nearly hourly, 2 hours, 90 kr), **Svartsö** (3/day, 2.5 hours, 110 kr),

and **Sandhamn** (1/day, Sat-Sun only, 3.5 hours). These destinations are all listed in Waxholmsbolaget's challenging-to-decipher schedule for the Middle Archipelago (Mellersta Skärgården). The same company has routes and schedules for the North and South Archipelago as well.

Cinderella Båtarna: This company focuses its coverage on the most popular destinations. Their ships—generally faster, more comfortable, and a little pricier than their rival's—leave from near Stockholm's Nybroplan, along Strandvägen (tel. 08/1200-4000, www.cinderellabatarna.com). Cinderella boats sail frequently (4/day Mon-Thu, 5/day Fri-Sun) from Stockholm to **Vaxholm** (50 minutes, 100 kr) and **Grinda** (1.25 hours, 120 kr). After Grinda, the line splits, going either to **Sandhamn** (from Stockholm: 1/day Mon-Thu, 2/day Fri-Sun, 2.75 hours, 150 kr), or Finnhamn, with a stop en route at **Svartsö** (from Stockholm: 2/day, 1.5 hours, 145 kr). Cinderella's fares are slightly cheaper off-season.

On Board: When you board, tell the conductor which island you're going to. Boats don't land at all of the smaller islands unless passengers have requested a stop. Hang on to your ticket, as you'll have to show it to disembark. Some boats have luggage-storage areas (ask when you board).

You can usually access the outdoor deck; if you can't get to the front deck (where the boats load and unload), head to the back. Or nab a window seat inside. For the best seat, with less sun and nicer views, I'd go POSH: Port Out, Starboard Home (on the left side leaving Stockholm, on the right side coming back). As you sail, a monitor on board shows the position of your boat as it motors through the islands.

Food: You can usually buy food on board, ranging from simple fare at snack bars (60-kr sandwiches and basic 85-100-kr meals) to elegant sea-view dinners at fancy restaurants (100-kr starters, 200-kr main dishes). If your boat has a top-deck restaurant and you want to combine your cruise with dinner, make a reservation as soon as you board. Once you have a table, it's yours for the whole trip, so you can simply claim your seat and enjoy the ride, circling back later to eat. You can also try calling ahead to reserve a table for a specific cruise (for Waxholmsbolaget, call 08/243-090; for Cinderella, call 08/1200-4000).

Helpful Hints

Opening Times: All the opening hours I list in this chapter are reliable only for peak season (mid-June–mid-Aug). The rest of the year, hours are flexible and completely weather-dependent. Outside the short summer season, many places close down entirely.

Money: Bring cash. The only ATMs are in Vaxholm; farther out, you'll wish you'd stocked up on cash in Stockholm. Fortunately, most vendors do accept credit cards.

Signal for Stop: At the boat landings or jetties on small islands, you'll notice a small signal tower (called a semaphore) that's used to let a passing boat know you want to be picked up. Pull the cord to spin the white disc and make it visible to the ship. Be sure to put it back before boarding the boat. At night, you signal with light—locals just use their mobile phones.

Weather: The weather on the islands is often better than in Stockholm. For island forecasts, check Götland's (the big island far to the south) instead of Stockholm's.

Local Drink: A popular drink here is *punsch,* a sweet fruit liqueur. Stately old buildings sometimes have *punsch-verandas,* little glassed-in upstairs porches where people traditionally would imbibe and chat.

Vaxholm

The self-proclaimed "gateway to the archipelago," Vaxholm (VAX-holm) is more developed and less charming than the other islands. Connected by bridge to Stockholm, it's practically a suburb, and not the place to commune with Swedish nature. But it also has an illustrious history as the anchor of Stockholm's naval defense network, and it couldn't be easier to reach (constant buses and boats from Stockholm). While Vaxholm isn't the rustic archipelago you might be looking for, you're almost certain to pass through here at some point on your trip. If you have some extra time, hop off the boat for a visit.

Getting There: Boats constantly shuttle between Stockholm's waterfront and Vaxholm (1-2/hour, 1.25 hours, 75-100 kr depending on boat company). **Bus #670** runs regularly from the Tekniska Högskolan T-bana stop in northern Stockholm to the center of Vaxholm (3/hour Mon-Fri, 2/hour Sat-Sun, 45-minute trip, 72 kr one-way—three zones). Unless you're on a tight budget, I'd take the boat for the scenery.

ARCHIPELAGO

Orientation to Vaxholm

(area code: 08)
Vaxholm, with about 11,000 people, is on the island of Vaxön, connected to the mainland (and Stockholm) by a series of bridges. Everything of interest is within a five-minute walk of the boat dock.

Arrival in Vaxholm

Ferries stop at Vaxholm's south harbor (Söderhamnen). The **bus** from Stockholm begins and ends at the bus stop called Söderhamnsplan, a few steps from the boats. To get your bearings, follow my self-guided walk. There are luggage lockers in the Waxholmsbolaget building on the waterfront. The handy electronic departure board (*Nästa Avgång* means "next departure") near the ticket office shows when boats are leaving. For more help, confirm your plans with the person at the ticket office.

Tourist Information

Vaxholm's good TI is well-stocked with brochures about Vaxholm itself, Stockholm, and the archipelago, and can help you with boat schedules (June-Aug Mon-Fri 10:00-18:00, Sat-Sun 10:00-16:00; May and Sept Mon-Fri 11:00-16:00, Sat-Sun 11:00-15:00; Oct-April Mon-Fri 10:00-15:00, Sat-Sun 10:00-14:00; in the Town Hall building on Rådhustorget, tel. 08/5413-1480, www.roslagen .se). They also have pay Internet access.

Self-Guided Walk

Welcome to Vaxholm

This 30-minute, two-part loop will take you to the most characteristic corners of Vaxholm. Begin at the boat dock—you can even start reading as you approach.

Waterfront: Dominating Vaxholm's waterfront is the big Art Nouveau Waxholms Hotell, dating from the early 20th century. Across the strait to the right is Vaxholm's stout fortress, a reminder of this town's strategic importance over the centuries.

With your back to the water, turn left and walk with the big hotel on your right-hand side. Notice the Waxholmsbolaget office building. Inside you can buy tickets, confirm boat schedules, or stow your bag in a locker. After the hamburger-and-hot-dog stand, you'll reach a roundabout. Just to your left is the stop for bus #670, connecting Vaxholm to Stockholm. Beyond that, a wooden walkway follows the seafront to the town's private boat harbor (Västerhamnen, or "west harbor"), where you can count sailboats and rent a bike.

But for now, continue straight up Vaxholm's appealing, shop-lined main street, Hamngatan. After one long block (notice the handy Coop/Konsum grocery store across the street), turn right up Rådhusgatan (following signs to *Rådhustorget*) to reach the town's main square. The TI is inside the big, yellow Town Hall building on your left. Continue kitty-corner across the square (toward the granite slope) and head downhill on a street leading to the...

Fishermen's Quarter: This Norrhamnen ("north harbor") is ringed by former fishermen's homes. Walk out to the dock and survey the charming wooden cottages. In the mid-19th century, Stockholmers considered Vaxholm's herring, called *strömming*,

top-quality. Caught fresh here, the herring could be rowed into the city in just eight hours and eaten immediately, while herring caught farther out on the archipelago, which had to be preserved in salt, lost its flavor.

As you look out to sea, you'll see a pale green building protruding on the left. This is the charming Hembygdsgården homestead museum, with a pleasant indoor-outdoor café. It's worth heading to this little point (even if the museum is closed, as it often is): As you face the water, go left about one block, then turn right down the gravel lane called Trädgårdsgatan (also marked for *Hembygdsgården*). At this corner, look for the *Strömmingslådan* ("herring shop") sign for the chance to buy what herring connoisseurs consider top-notch fish (summer only, Tue-Fri 10:00-16:00, Sat 10:00-14:00, closed Sun-Mon).

Continuing down Trädgårdsgatan lane, you'll run right into the **Hembygdsgården homestead.** The big house features an endearing museum showing simple, traditional fishermen lifestyles (free but donation requested, June-Aug Fri-Sun 12:00-16:00, plus Mon in July, otherwise closed). Next door is a fine café serving sweets and light meals with idyllic outdoor seating (both in front of and behind the museum—look around for your favorite perch, taking the wind direction into consideration). This is the best spot in town for coffee or lunch (see listing under "Sleeping and Eating in Vaxholm," later). From here, look across the inlet at the tiny beach (where we're heading next).

Backtrack to the fishermen's harbor, then continue straight uphill on Fiskaregatan road, and take the first left up the tiny gravel lane marked Vallgatan. This part of the walk takes you back in time, as you wander among old-fashioned wooden homes. At the end of the lane, head left; then, when you reach the water, go right along a path leading to a thriving little **sandy beach.** In good weather, this offers a fun chance to commune with Swedes at play. (In bad weather, it's hard to imagine anyone swimming or sunning here.)

When you're done relaxing, take the wooden stairs up to the top of the rock and **Battery Park** (Battcripark)—where giant artillery helped Vaxholm flex its defensive muscles in the late 19th century. As you crest the rock and enjoy the sea views, notice (on your right) the surviving semicircular tracks from those old artillery guns. With a range of 10 kilometers, the recoil from these powerful cannons could shatter glass in nearby houses. Before testing them, they'd play a bugle call to warn locals to stow away their valuables. More artifacts of these defenses are dug into the rock.

To head back to civilization, turn right before the embedded bunker (crossing more gun tracks and passing more fortifications on your left). As you leave the militarized zone, take a left at the fork, and the road will take you down to the embankment—just around the corner from where the boat docks, and our starting point. From along this stretch of embankment, you can catch a boat across the water to Vaxholm Fortress.

Sights in Vaxholm

Vaxholm Fortress and Museum (Vaxholms Kastell/ Vaxholms Fästnings Museum)—Vaxholm's only real attraction is the fortification just across the strait. While the town feels sleepy today, for centuries it was a crucial link in Sweden's nautical defense because it presided over the most convenient passage between Stockholm and the outer archipelago (and, beyond that, the Baltic Sea,

Finland, and Russia). The name "Vaxholm" means "Island of the Signal Fire," emphasizing the burg's strategic importance. In 1548, King Gustav Vasa decided to pin his chances on this location, ordering the construction of a fortress here and literally filling in other waterways, effectively making this the only way into or out of Stockholm...which it remained for 450 years. A village sprang up across the waterway to supply the fortress, and Vaxholm was born. The town's defenses successfully held off at least two major invasions (Christian IV of Denmark in 1612, and Peter the Great of Russia in 1719). Vaxholm's might gave Sweden's kings the peace of mind they needed to expand their capital to outlying islands— which means that the pint-size powerhouse of Vaxholm is largely to thank for Stockholm's island-hopping cityscape.

The current, "new" fortress dates from the mid-19th century, when an older castle was torn down and replaced with this imposing granite behemoth. During the 30 years it took to complete the fortress, the tools of warfare changed. Both defensively and offensively, the new fortress was obsolete before it was even completed. The thick walls were no match for the invention of shells (rather than cannonballs), and the high hatches used for attacking tall sailing vessels were useless against new, low-lying, monitor-style attack boats.

Today, the fortress welcomes guests to wander its tough little island and visit its museum. Presented chronologically on two floors (starting upstairs), the modern exhibit traces the military history of this fortress and of Sweden generally. It uses lots of models and mannequins, along with actual weaponry and artifacts, to tell the story right up to the 21st century. There's no English posted, but you can pick up the good English translations as you enter. It's as interesting as a museum about Swedish military history can be.

Cost and Hours: 50 kr, July-Aug daily 11:00-17:00, June daily 12:00-16:00, first and second Sat-Sun in Sept 11:00-17:00, closed off-season, tel. 08/5417-1890, www.vaxholmsfastning.se.

ARCHIPELAGO

Getting There: A ferry shuttles visitors back and forth from Vaxholm (50 kr round-trip, every 15 minutes when museum is open, catch the boat just around the corner and toward the fortress from where the big ferries put in). Once on the island, hike into the castle's inner courtyard and look to the left to find the museum entrance.

Sleeping and Eating in Vaxholm

Since Vaxholm is so close to Stockholm, there's little reason to sleep here. But in a pinch, Waxholms is the only hotel in town.

$$$ Waxholms Hotell's stately Art Nouveau facade dominates the town's waterfront. Inside are 42 pleasant rooms with classy old-fashioned furnishings (peak-season Sb-1,400, Db-1,750; weekends/July Sb-1,100 kr, Db-1,400 kr; free Wi-Fi, loud music some nights in summer—ask what's on and request a quiet room if necessary, Hamngatan 2, tel. 08/5413-0150, fax 08/5413-1376, www.waxholmshotell.se, info@waxholmshotell.se). The hotel has a grill restaurant outside in summer and a fancy dining room inside.

Hembygdsgården ("Homestead Garden") **Café** is Vaxholm's most tempting eatery, serving "summer lunches" (salads and sandwiches) and homemade sweets, with delightful outdoor seating around the Homestead Museum in Vaxholm's characteristic fishermen's quarter. Anette's lingonberry muffins are a treat (40-75-kr light meals, daily mid-June-Aug 11:00-18:00, May-mid-June 11:00-16:00, closed Sept-April, tel. 08/5413-1980).

Sleep Code

(6 kr = about $1, country code: 46, area code: 08)
S = Single, **D** = Double/Twin, **T** = Triple, **Q** = Quad, **b** = bathroom, **s** = shower. Unless otherwise noted, all of my listings accept credit cards and include big breakfast buffets. Everyone speaks English.

To help you sort easily through these listings, I've divided the accommodations into three categories, based on the price for a standard double room with bath during high season:

$$$ Higher Priced—Most rooms 1,500 kr or more.
  $$ Moderately Priced—Most rooms between 1,000-1,500 kr.
    $ Lower Priced—Most rooms 1,000 kr or less.

Prices can change without notice; verify the hotel's current rates online or by email. For other updates, see www .ricksteves.com/update.

Grinda

The rustic, traffic-free isle of Grinda—half retreat, half resort—combines back-to-nature archipelago remoteness with easy proximity to Stockholm. The island is a tasteful gaggle of hotel buildings idyllically situated amid Swedish nature—walking paths, beaches, trees, and slabs of glacier-carved granite sloping into the sea. Since Grinda is a nature preserve (owned by the Stockholm Archipelago Foundation, or Skärgårdsstiftelsen), only a few families actually live here. There's no real town. But in the summer, Grinda becomes a magnet for day-tripping urbanites, which can make it quite crowded. Adding to its appeal is the nostalgia it holds for many Stockholmers, who fondly recall when this was a summer camp island. In a way, with red-and-white cottages bunny-hopping up its gentle hills and a stately old inn anchoring its center, it retains that vibe today.

Orientation to Grinda

(area code: 08)
Grinda is small and easy to manage. It's a little wider than a mile in each direction; you can walk from end to end in a half-hour. Its main settlement—the historic Wärdshus building (a busy hub of tourist activities), hotel, and related amenities—sits next to its harbor, where private yachts and sailboats put in. Public ferries use one of two docks, at opposite ends of the island: Most use Södra Grinda to the south (nearest the hostel and cottages), while a few use Norra Grinda to the north (closer to the campground). From either of these, it's about a 10- to 15-minute walk to the action. Everything on the island is owned and operated by the same company; fortunately, it does a tasteful job of managing the place to keep the island's relaxing personality intact.

Major points of interests are well-signposted in Swedish: *Södra Bryggan* (south dock), *Norra Bryggan* (north dock), *Värdshus* (hotel at the heart of the island), *Gästhamn* (guest harbor); *Affär* (general store); *stuga/stugby* (cottage/s); *Grindastigen* (nature trail); and *Tältplats* (campground).

Tourist Information
The red cottage marked *Expedition* greets arriving visitors just up the hill from the Södra Grinda ferry dock. The staff answers ques-

tions, and the cottage serves as a small shop, a place to rent kayaks or saunas, and a reception desk for the island's cottages and hostel (mid-June-mid-Aug daily 9:00-18:00; shoulder season Mon-Fri 10:00-16:00, Sat 10:00-18:00, Sun 10:00-14:00; general info tel. 08/5424-9491, www.skargardsstiftelsen.se).

Sights in Grinda

Grinda is made to order for strolling through the woods, taking a dip, picnicking, and communing with Swedish nature. Watch

the boats bob in the harbor and work on your Baltic tan. You can simply stick to the gravel trails connecting the island's buildings, or for more nature, take the Grindastigen trail, which loops to the far end of the island and back in less than an hour (signposted from near the Wärdshus).

You can also rent a kayak or rent the private little sauna hut bobbing in the harbor. There's no bike rental here—and the island is a bit too small to keep a serious biker busy—but you could bring one on the boat from Stockholm.

As you stroll, you might spot a few haggard-looking tents through the trees. The right to pitch a tent here was established by the Swedish government during World War II, to give the downtrodden a cheap place to sleep. Those permissions are still valid, inherited, bought, and sold, which means that Grinda has a thriving community of tent-dwelling locals who camp out here all summer long (April-Oct). While some may be the descendants of those original hobos, these days they choose this lifestyle and live as strange little barnacles attached to Grinda. Once each summer they have a progressive tent-crawl bender before heading to the Wärdshus to blow a week's food budget on a fancy meal.

The island just across from the Södra Grinda dock (to the right) is Viggsö, where the members of ABBA have summer cottages and wrote many of their biggest hits.

Sleeping in Grinda

(6 kr = about $1, country code: 46, area code 08)
You have various options, in increasing order of rustic charm: hotel, hostel, and cottages. You can reserve any of these through the Wärdshus. This hub of operations has a restaurant, bar, free Wi-Fi, and conference facilities (tel. 08/5424-9491, www.grinda .se, info@grinda.se).

ARCHIPELAGO

Grinda is busiest in the summer, when tourists fill its hotel; in spring and fall, it mostly hosts conferences. If sleeping at the hostel or cottages, arrange arrival details (you'll probably pick up your keys at the *Expedition* shed near the dock). The hostel and cottages charge extra for bed linens. If you have a tent, you can pitch it on the island for 80 kr.

$$$ Grinda Hotel rents 30 rooms in four buildings just above the Wärdshus. These are modern, comfortable, and made for relaxing, intentionally lacking distractions such as TVs or phones (Sb-1,400 kr, Db-1,800 kr, larger suite-2,440 kr, 120 kr less per person if you skip breakfast, 20 percent cheaper if you stay more than 3 nights, extra bed-350 kr, if dining at the restaurant the "Wärdshus package" will save you a few kronor).

$ The 27 cottages—most near the Södra Grinda ferry dock—are rentable, offering a rustic retreat (kitchenettes but no running water, shared bathroom facilities outside). From mid-June to mid-August, these come with a one-week minimum and cost more (2-bed cottage-3,000 kr/week, 4-bed cottage-3,500 kr/week, 6-bed cottage-4,000 kr; at other times rentable by the night: 2-bed-1,000 kr, 4-bed-1,100 kr, 6-bed-1,300 kr).

$ Grinda Hostel (Vandrarheim) is the place to sleep if you wish you'd gone to Swedish summer camp as a kid. The 44 bunks are in simple two- and four-bed cottages, surrounding a pair of fire pits (300 kr/bed regardless of room size, great shared kitchen/dining hall). A small pebbly beach and a basic sauna are nearby.

Eating in Grinda

All your options (aside from bringing your own picnic from Stockholm) are run by the hotel. Fortunately, there are choices for each price range.

Grinda Wärdshus, the inn at the center of the complex, has a good restaurant that combines rural island charm with fine food. You can choose between traditional Swedish meals and contemporary international dishes. Servings are small but thoughtfully designed to be delicious. Eat in the woody dining room or on the terrace out front (1,395 kr covers dinner and room, 180-300-kr main dishes, 115-165-kr starters; late June-Aug daily 12:00-24:00; off-season Fri 17:00-23:00, Sat 12:00-23:00, Sun 12:00-18:00, closed Mon-Thu; also closed Fri Dec-early March).

Grindas Framficka ("Grinda's Front Pocket") is a pleasant bistro that serves up basic but tasty food (such as fishburgers and grilled shrimp) right along the guest harbor. Order at the counter, then choose a table to wait for your food (100-140-kr dishes, early June-mid-Aug daily 11:00-22:00, otherwise sporadically open in good weather—especially weekends).

The **general store and café** (Lanthandel) just below the Wärdshus is the place to rustle up some picnic fixings. You'll also find coffee to go, ice cream, and 40-kr "one-time grills" for a disposable barbecue (early June-mid-Aug daily 8:00-18:00; shoulder season Sat 10:00-18:00, Sun 10:00-16:00, open sporadically Mon-Fri).

Svartsö

The remote and lesser-known isle of Svartsö (svert-show, literally "Black Island"), a short hop beyond Grinda, is the "Back Door"

option of the bunch. Unlike Grinda, Svartsö is home to a real community; islanders have their own school and library. But with only 80 year-round residents, the old generation had to specialize. Each person learned a skill to fill a niche in the community—one guy was a carpenter, the next was a plumber, the next was an electrician, and so on. While the island is less trampled than the others in this chapter (just one B&B and a great restaurant), it is reasonably well-served by ferries. Svartsö feels remote and potentially even boring for those who aren't wowed by simply strolling through meadows. But it's ideal for those who want to slow down and immerse themselves in nature.

Orientation to Svartsö

The island, about five miles long and a half-mile wide, has three docks. The main one, at the southwestern tip, is called Alsvik (with the general store and restaurant). Halfway up is Skälvik (near the B&B), and at the northeastern end is Söderboudd. Most boats stop at Alsvik, but if you want to go to a different dock, you can request a stop (ask the conductor on board, or use the semaphore signal at the dock).

At the **Alsvik dock,** the great little general store, called Svartsö Lanthandel, sells anything you could need and also acts as the town TI, post office, and liquor store (mid-June-mid-Aug

Mon-Fri 9:00-19:30, Sat-Sun 10:00-18:00; mid-May-mid-June Mon-Thu 9:00-17:30, Fri 9:00-19:30, Sat-Sun 10:00-14:00; shorter off-season, tel. 08/5424-7325, run by friendly Matte Hedelin). You can rent bikes here; call ahead to reserve in busy times. The little café on the dock sells drinks and light food, and rents cottages (shared showers and toilets, tel. 08/5424-7110).

The island has a few paved lanes and almost no traffic. Residents own three-wheeled utility motorbikes for hauling things to and from the ferry landing. The interior consists of little more than trees. With an hour or so, you can bike across the island and back, enjoying the mellow landscape and chatting with the friendly big-city people who've found their perfect escape.

Svartsö hosts the school for this part of the archipelago. Because Swedish law guarantees the right to education, even kids living on remote islands are transported to class. A school boat trundles from island to island each morning to collect kids headed for the school on Svartsö. If the weather is bad, a hover-craft retrieves them. If it's really bad, and all of the snow days have been used up, a helicopter takes the kids to school.

Eating in Svartsö

If you leave the Alsvik dock to the right and walk five minutes up the hill, you'll find the excellent **Svartsö Krog** restaurant. Opened by a pair of can-do foodies who also run a top-end butcher shop at a Stockholm market hall, this place has a deep respect for the sanctity of meat. Specializing in well-constructed, ingredient-driven dishes, the restaurant brings Stockholm culinary sophisti-cation to a castaway island. Choose one of the three eating zones (each with the same menu): outside, the upscale dining room, or in the original pub interior (an Old West-feeling tavern that the new owner has kept as-is to respect the old-timers). The menu is pricey but good (130-160-kr starters, 200-300-kr main dishes). Their specialty is "golden entrecôte," grilled steak that's been aged for eight weeks (figure a hefty 580 kr but potentially worth it for meat-lovers; June-Aug daily 11:00-1:00 in the morning; May and Sept Thu 16:00-1:00, Fri 15:00-1:00, Sat 12:00-1:00, Sun 12:00-18:00, closed Mon-Wed; closed Oct-April; tel. 08/5424-7255).

Sandhamn

Out on the distant fringe of the archipelago—the last stop before Finland—sits the proud village of Sandhamn (on the island of

Sandön). Literally "Sand Harbor," this is where the glacier got hung up and kept on churning away, grinding stone into sand. The town has a long history as an important and posh place. In 1897, the Royal Swedish Sailing Society built its clubhouse here, putting Sandhamn on the map as the yachting center of the Baltic—Sweden's answer to Nantucket. It remains an extremely popular stop for boaters—from wealthy yachties to sailboat racers—as well as visitors simply seeking a break from the big city.

You'll find two halves to Sandhamn: In the shadow of that still-standing iconic yacht clubhouse is a ritzy resort/party zone throbbing with big-money nautical types. But just a few steps away, around the harbor, is an idyllic time-warp Old Town of colorfully painted shiplap cottages tucked between tranquil pine groves. While most tourists come here for the resort, the quieter part of Sandhamn holds the real appeal.

Orientation to Sandhamn

(area code: 08)

The island of Sandön feels stranded on the edge of the archipelago, rather than immersed in it. On its sheltered side is the town of

Sandhamn. Though it's far from Stockholm, Sandhamn is very popular. During the peak of summer (mid-June through late August), it's extremely crowded. Expect to stand in line, and call ahead for restaurant reservations. But even during these times,

the Old Town is relatively peaceful and pleasant to explore. If the weather's decent, shoulder season is delightful (though it can be busy on weekends).

Sandhamn's hopes of opening a TI may produce one in time for your visit, but don't count on it. There's also no ATM in Sandhamn, so bring cash (or use your credit card).

Self-Guided Tour

Welcome to Sandhamn

To get your bearings from the ferry dock, take the following tour. Begin by facing out to sea.

As you look out to the little point across from the dock, notice the big yellow building. In the 18th century, this was built as the **pilot house.** Because the archipelago is so treacherous to navigate—with its tens of thousands of islands and skerries, not to mention untold numbers of hidden underwater rocks—locals don't trust outsiders to bring their boats here. So passing ships unfamiliar with these waters were required

to pick up a local captain (or "pilot") to take them safely all the way to Stockholm. The tradition continues today. The orange boats marked *pilot,* moored below the house, ferry loaner captains to oncoming ships. And, since this is the point of entry into Sweden, foreign ships can also be processed by customs here.

The little red shed just in front of the pilot house is home to a humble **town museum** that's open sporadically in the summer, featuring exhibits on Sandhamn's history and some seafaring tales. Just below that, notice the waterfront red barn with the *T* sign. The owner of this boat-repair shop erected this marker for Stockholm's T-bana just for fun.

Just above the barn, look for the yellow building with the blue letters spelling **Sandhamns Värdshus.** This traditional inn, built in the late 17th century, housed sailors while they waited here to set out to sea. During that time, Stockholm had few exports, so ships that brought and unloaded cargo there came to Sandhamn to load up their holds with its abundant sand as ballast. Today the inn still serves good food (see "Eating in Sandhamn," later).

Stretching to the left of the inn are the quaint storefronts of most of Sandhamn's **eateries** (those that aren't affiliated with the big hotel)—bakery, deli, and grocery store, all of them humble but just right for a simple bite or picnic shopping. Local merchants enjoy a pleasantly symbiotic relationship. Rather than try to compete with each other, they attempt to complement what the next shop sells—each one finding just the right niche. (For details, see "Eating in Sandhamn," later.)

The area stretching beyond these storefronts is Sandhamn's **Old Town**—a maze of wooden cottages that's an absolute delight to explore (and easily the best activity in town). Only 50 of Sandhamn's homes (of around 450) are occupied by year-rounders.

The rest are summer cottages of wealthy Stockholmers, or bunk-houses for seasonal workers in the tourist industry. Most locals live at the farthest-flung (and therefore least desirable) locations. Imagine the impact of 100,000 annual visitors on this little town.

Where the jetty meets the island, notice (on the right) the old-fashioned telephone box with the fancy *Rikstelefon* logo. It

contains the island's lone working pay phone. Just to the right of the phone box, you can see the back of the town's bulletin board, where locals post their classified ads. To the left at the base of the dock is Sandhamns Kiosk, a newsstand selling local and international publications (as well as candy and ice cream). A bit farther to the left, the giant red building with the turret on top is the **yacht clubhouse** that put Sandhamn on the map, and still entertains the upper crust today with a hotel, several restaurants, spa, mini-golf course, outdoor pool, and more. You'll see its proud SSS-plus-crown logo (standing for Svenska Segelsällskapet—Swedish Sailing Society) all over town. In the 1970s, the building was owned by a notorious mobster who made meth in the basement, then smuggled it out beneath the dock to sailboats moored in the harbor.

Spinning a bit farther to the left, back to where you started, survey the island across the strait (Lökholmen). Just above the trees, notice the copper dome of an observatory that was built by this island's eccentric German oil-magnate owner in the early 20th century. He also built a small castle (not quite visible from here) for his kids to play in.

For a narrated stroll to another fine viewpoint, walk into town and turn left along the water. After about 50 yards, a sign on the right points up a narrow lane to *Post*. This unassuming gravel path is actually one of Sandhamn's most important streets, with the post office, police department (which handles only paperwork—real crimes are deferred to the Stockholm PD), and doctor (who visits town every second Wednesday). While Sandhamn feels remote, it's served—like other archipelago communities—by a crack emergency-response network that can dispatch a medical boat, or in extreme cases, helicopter. With top-notch hospitals in Stockholm just a 10-minute chopper ride away, locals figure that

ARCHIPELAGO

if you have an emergency here, you might just make it to the doctor faster than if you're trying to make it through congested city streets in an ambulance. At the end of this lane, notice the giant hill of the town's namesake sand.

Continuing along the main tree-lined harborfront strip, you can't miss the signs directing yachters to the *toalett* (toilet) and *sopor* (garbage dump). Then you'll pass the Sandhamns Guiderna office, a **travel agency** where you can rent bikes, kayaks, and fishing gear. (If they've managed to open a TI in time for your visit, this is where you'll find it; travel agency tel. 08/640-8040.) Just after that is the barn for the volunteer fire department (Brandstation). With all the wooden buildings in town, fire is a concern—one reason why Sandhamn restricts camping (and campfires).

Go beneath the skyway connecting the big red hotel to its modern annex. Then veer uphill (right) at the *Badstranden Trouville* sign, looking down at the mini-golf course. After you crest the top of the hill, on the left is a big, flat expanse of rock nicknamed Dansberget ("Dancing Rock") because it once hosted community dances with a live orchestra. Walk out to enjoy fine **views** of the Baltic Sea—from here, boaters can set

sail for Finland, Estonia, and St. Petersburg, Russia. Looking out to the horizon, notice the three lighthouse towers poking up from the sea, used to guide ships to this gateway to the archipelago. The finish line for big boat races stretches across this gap (from the little house on the point to your left). In summer, this already busy town gets even more jammed with visitors, thanks to the frequent sailing races that end here. The biggest annual competition is the Götlandrunt, a round-trip from here to the island of Götland. In 2009, Sandhamn was proud to be one of just 10 checkpoints on the Volvo Ocean Race, a nine-month race around the world that called mostly at bigger cities (such as Boston, Singapore, and Rio). It was such a huge deal here that locals are aghast at the thought that anyone hasn't heard about it.

Our walk is finished. You can head back into town. Or, to hit the beach, continue another 15 minutes to Trouville beach (explained below).

Sights in Sandhamn

Beaches (Stränder)—True to its name, Sandön ("Sandy Island") has some of the archipelago's rare sandy beaches. The closest and local favorite is the no-name beach tucked in a cove just behind the

Old Town (walk through the community from the main boat dock, then follow the cove around to the little sandy stretch).

The most popular—which can be quite crowded in summer—is Trouville beach, at the opposite end of the island from Sandhamn (about a 20-minute walk). Two swathes of sand are marked off by rocks stretching toward Finland. To find it, walk behind the big red hotel and take the right, uphill fork (marked with the low-profile *Badstranden Trouville* sign) to the "Dancing Rock," then proceed along the road. Take a left at the fork by the tennis courts, then walk about 10 minutes through a mysterious-feeling forest until you reach a little settlement of red cottages. Take a right at the fork (look up for the *Till Stranden* sign), and then, soon after, follow the middle fork (along the plank walks) right to the beach zone.

Sleeping in Sandhamn

(6 kr = about $1, country code: 46, area code 08)

Sandhamn has a pair of very expensive top-end hotels, a basic but comfortable B&B, and little else. If you're sleeping on Sandhamn, the B&B is the best choice.

$$$ Sands Hotell is a stylish splurge sitting proudly at the top of town. While oriented mostly to conferences and private parties, its 19 luxurious rooms also welcome commoners in the summer (Sb-2,200 kr, Db-2,500 kr, free Wi-Fi, elevator, spa in basement, tel. 08/5715-3020, www.sandshotell.se, info@sands hotell.se).

$$$ Sandhamns Seglarhotellet rents 79 nautical-themed rooms in a modern annex behind the old yacht club building (where you'll find the reception). The rooms are fine, but the prices are sky-high (Sb/Db-2,390 kr, 200 kr more for balcony, extra bed-400 kr, free Wi-Fi, loud music from disco inside the clubhouse—light sleepers should ask for a quieter back room, great gym and pool area in basement, tel. 08/5745-0400, www.sandhamn.com, reception@sandhamn.com).

$ Sandhamns Värdshus B&B rents five rustic but tasteful, classically Swedish rooms in an old mission house buried deep in the colorful Old Town. To melt into Sandhamn and get away from the yachties, sleep here (S-795 kr, D-1,290 kr, mostly twins, all rooms share WC and shower, tiny cottage with its own bathroom

ARCHIPELAGO

for same price, includes breakfast, reception is at the restaurant—see below, tel. 08/5715-3051, www.sandhamns-vardshus.se, info @sandhamns-vardshus.se). The rooms are above a reception hall that is rented out for events, but after 22:00, quiet time kicks in.

Eating in Sandhamn

In the Old Town

Sandhamn's most appealing eateries are along the Old Town side of the harbor.

Sandhamns Värdshus, right on the water, is the town's best eatery. They serve traditional Swedish food in three separate dining zones (which mostly share the same menu, but each also has its own specials): out on an inviting deck overlooking the water; upstairs in a salty dining room with views; or downstairs in a simple pub (100-150-kr starters, 100-250-kr main dishes, pub serves cheap lunch deal for 69-89 kr; Easter-Oct daily 11:00-22:30, Nov-Easter Mon-Sat closed 14:00-17:00 & after 21:00, Sun 11:00-18:00; reservations possible only in restaurant—otherwise first-come first-served, tel. 08/5715-3051).

To grab a bite or assemble a picnic, browse through these smaller eateries (listed in the order you'll reach them from the boat dock): **Westerbergs Livsmedel** grocery store has basic supplies (Mon-Fri 10:00-13:00 & 16:00-18:00, Sat 10:00-15:00, Sun 10:00-13:00). **Dykarbaren Café** serves meals with indoor and outdoor seating (110-175-kr lunches, 240-300-kr dinners, summer daily 11:00-24:00; May-mid-June and mid-Aug-Sept Wed-Sat 11:00-15:00 & 18:00-24:00, Sun 11:00-15:00, closed Mon-Tue and off-season; tel. 08/5715-3554). **Sandhamns Deli** is a bright, innovative shop where you can buy 45-kr sandwiches and salads, a wide array of meats for grilling, cheeses, cold cuts, drinks, fresh produce, and other high-quality picnic fixings (daily in summer 10:00-19:00, later in good weather, mobile 0709-650-300). Just around the corner (uphill from the harbor and behind the Värdsgasthus) is **Sandhamns Bageriet,** a popular bakery/café serving coffee, sweet rolls, and 50-kr sandwiches (daily in summer 8:00-17:00, "self-service café" opens at 7:00).

Among the Yachties

Sandhamns Seglarhotellet has several eateries, open to guests and non-guests. Out on the dock is the Café Seglar'n, an American-style grill with a take-out window and outdoor tables (40-80-kr

ARCHIPELAGO

dishes, 150-kr combo meals, open in summer in good weather only). Upstairs in the building's main ballroom is an eatery serving good but pricey Swedish and international food. There are two parts—the cheaper, mellow bistro (100-150-kr starters, 200-250-kr main dishes, traditional daily lunch special for 150 kr), and the fancier restaurant (150-200-kr starters, 185-300-kr main dishes). Both parts enjoy fine sea views, and they meet at the bar/dance hall zone in the middle (with loud disco music until 2:00 in the morning nearly nightly in summer). Down on the ground floor is a pub/nightclub (tel. 08/5745-0421).

PRACTICALITIES

This section covers just the basics on traveling in this region (for much more information, see *Rick Steves' Scandinavia*). You'll find free advice on specific topics at www.ricksteves.com/tips.

Money

Sweden uses the Swedish kroner: 1 krona equals about $0.17. To roughly convert prices in kroner to dollars, divide prices by 6 (100 kr = about $16). Check www.oanda.com for the latest exchange rates.

The standard way for travelers to get kroner is to withdraw money from a cash machine (ATM) using a debit or credit card, ideally with a Visa or MasterCard logo. Before departing, call your bank or credit-card company: Confirm that your card will work overseas, ask about international transaction fees, and alert them that you'll be making withdrawals in Europe.

Dealing with "Chip and PIN": Much of Northern Europe (including Sweden) is adopting a "chip-and-PIN" system for credit cards. These "smartcards" come with an embedded microchip, and cardholders enter a PIN code instead of signing a receipt. If your US card is rejected at a store, a cashier will probably be able to process your card the old-fashioned way. A few merchants might insist on the PIN code—making it helpful for you to know the code for your credit card (ask your credit-card company before you go). The easiest solution is to pay for your purchases with cash you've withdrawn from an ATM. Your US credit card may not be accepted at automated pay points, such as ticket machines at train and subway stations, parking garages, luggage lockers, and self-serve pumps at gas stations. But in Sweden, I've found that my US credit card will usually work in these machines, as long as I enter the PIN when the machine asks for the "kod."

To keep your valuables safe, wear a money belt. But if you do lose your credit or debit card, report the loss immediately to the respective global customer-assistance centers. Use this toll-free number in Sweden—020-799-111—to place a collect call to these 24-hour US numbers: Visa (410/581-9994), MasterCard (636/722-7111), and American Express (623/492-8427).

Phoning

Smart travelers use the telephone to reserve or reconfirm rooms, reserve restaurants, get directions, research transportation connections, confirm tour times, phone home, and lots more.

To call Sweden from the US or Canada: Dial 011-46 and then the area code (minus its initial zero) and local number. (The 011 is our international access code, and 46 is Sweden's country code.)

To call Sweden from a European country: Dial 00-46 followed the area code (minus its initial zero) and local number. (The 00 is Europe's international access code.)

To call within Sweden: If you're dialing within an area code, just dial the local number; but if you're calling outside your area code, you have to dial both the area code (which starts with a 0) and the local number.

Tips on Phoning: To make calls in Sweden, you can buy two different types of phone cards—international or insertable—sold locally at newsstands. Cheap international phone cards, which work with a scratch-to-reveal PIN code, allow you to call home to the US for pennies a minute, and also work for domestic calls. You can use these cards from any phone, including the one in your hotel room, but some hotels charge for calls to the "toll-free" access line (ask before you dial). Insertable phone cards, which must be inserted into public pay phones, are reasonable for calls within Sweden (and work for international calls as well, though not as cheaply as the international phone cards). Note that insertable phone cards—and most international phone cards—work only in the country where you buy them. Calling from your hotel-room phone *without* using an international phone card is usually expensive.

A mobile phone—whether an American one that works in Europe, or a European one you buy when you arrive—is handy, but can be pricey. For more on phoning, see www.ricksteves.com/phoning.

Making Hotel Reservations

To ensure the best value, I recommend reserving rooms in advance, particularly during peak season. Email the hotelier with the following key pieces of information: number and type of rooms; number of nights; date of arrival; date of departure; and any special requests. (For a sample form, see www.ricksteves.com/

reservation.) Use the European style for writing dates: day/month/ year. For example, for a two-night stay in July, you could request: "1 double room for 2 nights, arrive 16/07/12, depart 18/07/12." Hotcliers typically ask for your credit-card number as a deposit.

In these times of economic uncertainty, some hotels are willing to deal to attract guests—try emailing several to ask their best price. Most Scandinavian business hotels use "dynamic pricing," which means they change the room rate depending on demand—just like the airlines change their fares. This makes it extremely difficult to predict what you will pay. For many hotels, I list a range of prices. If the rate you're offered is at or near the bottom of my printed range, it's likely a good deal. In general, hotel prices can soften if you do any of the following: offer to pay cash, stay at least three nights, or travel off-season. You can also try asking for a cheaper room (for example, with a bathroom down the hall), or offer to skip breakfast. In Stockholm, business-class hotels drop prices to attract tourists with summer rates (mid-June through mid-August) and weekend rates (Friday and Saturday, but not Sunday).

Eating

Restaurants are often expensive. Alternate between picnics (outside or in your hotel or hostel); cheap, forgettable, but filling cafeteria or fast-food fare ($20 per person); and atmospheric, carefully chosen restaurants popular with locals ($35 per person and up). Ethnic eateries—Turkish, Greek, Italian, and Asian—offer a good value and a break from Swedish food.

If you want to enjoy a combination of picnics and restaurant meals on your trip, you'll save money by eating in restaurants at lunch (when there's usually a daily special—*dagens rätt*—and food is generally cheaper), then picnicking for dinner.

The *smörgåsbord* is a revered Scandinavian culinary tradition. Seek it out at least once during your visit. Begin with the fish dishes, along with boiled potatoes and *knäckebröd* (Swedish crisp bread). Then move on to salads, egg dishes, and various cold cuts. Next it's meatball time! Pour on some gravy as well as a spoonful of lingonberry sauce. Still hungry? Make a point to sample the Nordic cheeses and the racks of traditional desserts, cakes, and custards.

Hotel breakfasts are a huge and filling buffet, generally included but occasionally a $10-or-so option. It usually features fruit, cereal, various milks, breads, crackers, cold cuts, pickled herring, caviar paste, and boiled eggs.

In Sweden, most alcohol is sold only at state-run liquor stores called Systembolaget (though weak beer is available at supermarkets). To avoid extremely high restaurant prices for alcohol, many Swedes—and tourists—buy their wine, beer, or spirits at a store and then drink at a public square; this is legal and openly practiced.

One local specialty is *akvavit*, a strong, vodka-like spirit distilled from potatoes and flavored with anise, caraway, or other herbs and spices—then drunk ice-cold. *Lakka* is a syrupy-sweet liqueur made from cloudberries, the small orange berries grown in the Arctic.

Service: Good service is relaxed (slow to an American). When you want the bill, say, *"Kan jag få notan, tack."* Throughout Sweden, a service charge is included in your bill, so there's no need to leave an additional tip. In fancier restaurants or for great service, round up the bill (about 5 percent of the total check).

Transportation

By Train and Bus: Trains cover many Scandinavian destinations. If you're traveling beyond Stockholm and want to see if a railpass could save you money, check www.ricksteves.com/rail. If you're buying tickets as you go, note that prices can fluctuate. To research train schedules and fares, visit the Swedish train website: www.sj.se. Nearly any long-distance train ride requires you to make a reservation before boarding (the day before is usually fine).

Don't overlook long-distance buses (e.g., between Stockholm and Oslo), which are usually slower than trains but have considerably cheaper and more predictable fares. Sweden's biggest bus carrier is Swebus (www.swebus.se).

By Car: It's cheaper to arrange most car rentals from the US. For tips on your insurance options, see www.ricksteves.com/cdw, and for route planning, consult www.viamichelin.com. Bring your driver's license. Local road etiquette is similar to that in the US. Use your headlights day and night; it's required in most of Scandinavia. A car is a worthless headache in Stockholm—there's a congestion tax to enter the city center on weekdays. If you must drive into the city, park it safely (get tips from your hotelier).

By Boat: Boats are romantic, scenic, and sometimes the most efficient—or only—way to link destinations in coastal Sweden. Note that short-distance ferries may take only cash, not credit cards. Advance reservations are recommended when using overnight boats in summer or on weekends to link Stockholm with Helsinki (www.vikingline.fi and www.tallinksilja.com). For cruising the nearby islands, see the Stockholm's Archipelago chapter.

Helpful Hints

Emergency Help: To summon the **police** or an **ambulance,** dial 112. For passport problems, call the **US Embassy** (in Stockholm: tel. 08/783-5375; passport services available Mon–Fri 9:00–11:00, http://stockholm.usembassy.gov). For information on what to do in case of theft or loss, see www.ricksteves.com/help. For other concerns, get advice from your hotelier.

Time: Europe uses the 24-hour clock. It's the same through

12:00 noon, then keep going: 13:00, 14:00, and so on. Sweden is six/nine hours ahead of the East/West Coasts of the US.

Holidays and Festivals: Europe celebrates many holidays, which can close sights and attract crowds (book hotel rooms ahead). For information on holidays and festivals in Sweden, check the Scandinavia Tourist Board website: www.goscandinavia.com. For a simple list showing major—though not all—events, see www.ricksteves.com/festivals.

Numbers and Stumblers: What Americans call the second floor of a building is the first floor in Europe. Europeans write dates as day/month/year, so Christmas is 25/12/12. Commas are decimal points and vice versa—a dollar and a half is 1,50, and there are 5.280 feet in a mile. Europe uses the metric system: A kilogram is 2.2 pounds; a liter is about a quart; and a kilometer is six-tenths of a mile.

Resources from Rick Steves

This Snapshot guide is excerpted from the latest edition of *Rick Steves' Scandinavia,* which is one of more than 30 titles in my series of guidebooks on European travel. I also produce a public television series, *Rick Steves' Europe,* and a public radio show, *Travel with Rick Steves.* My website, www.ricksteves.com, offers free travel information, a Graffiti Wall for travelers' comments, guidebook updates, my travel blog, an online travel store, and information on European railpasses and our tours of Europe. If you're bringing a mobile device on your trip, you can download free information from Rick Steves Audio Europe, featuring podcasts of my radio shows, free audio tours of major sights in Europe, and travel interviews about Sweden (downloadable via www.ricksteves.com/audioeurope, iTunes, or the Rick Steves Audio Europe free smartphone app).

Additional Resources

Tourist Information: www.goscandinavia.com
Passports and Red Tape: www.travel.state.gov
Packing List: www.ricksteves.com/packlist
Travel Insurance: www.ricksteves.com/insurance
Cheap Flights: www.skyscanner.net
Airplane Carry-on Restrictions: www.tsa.gov/travelers
Updates for This Book: www.ricksteves.com/update

How Was Your Trip?

If you'd like to share your tips, concerns, and discoveries after using this book, please fill out the survey at www.ricksteves.com/feedback. Thanks in advance—it helps a lot.

Swedish Survival Phrases

Swedish pronunciation (especially the vowel sounds) can be tricky for Americans to say, and there's quite a bit of variation across the country; listen closely to locals and imitate, or ask for help. The most difficult Swedish sound is *sj*, which sounds roughly like a guttural "*hw*" (made in your throat); however, like many sounds, this is pronounced differently in various regions—for example, Stockholmers might say it more like "shw."

Hello. (formal)	**Goddag!**	goh-DAH
Hi. / Bye. (informal)	**Hej. / Hej då.**	hey / hey doh
Do you speak English?	**Talar du engelska?**	TAH-lahr doo ENG-ehl-skah
Yes. / No.	**Ja. / Nej.**	yaw / nay
Please.	**Snälla. / Tack.***	SNEHL-lah / tack
Thank you (very much).	**Tack (så mycket).**	tack (soh MEE-keh)
You're welcome.	**Ingen orsak.**	EENG-ehn OOR-sahk
Can I help you?	**Kan jag hjälpa dig?**	kahn yaw JEHL-pah day
Excuse me.	**Ursäkta.**	OOR-sehk-tah
(Very) good.	**(Mycket) bra.**	(MEE-keh) brah
Goodbye. (formal)	**Adjö.**	ah-YEW
one / two	**en / två**	ehn / tvoh
three / four	**tre / fyra**	treh / FEE-rah
five / six	**fem / sex**	fehm / sehks
seven / eight	**sju / åtta**	hwoo / OH-tah
nine / ten	**nio / tio**	NEE-oh / TEE-oh
hundred	**hundra**	HOON-drah
thousand	**tusen**	TEW-sehn
How much?	**Hur mycket?**	hewr MEE-keh
local currency: (Swedish) kronor	**(Svenske) kronor**	(svehn-SKEH) KROH-nor
Where is...?	**Var finns...?**	vahr feens
..the toilet	**...toaletten**	toh-ah-LEH-tehn
men	**man**	mahn
women	**kvinna**	KVEE-nah
water / coffee	**vatten / kaffe**	VAH-tehn / KAH-feh
beer / wine	**öl / vin**	url / veen
Cheers!	**Skål!**	skohl
The bill, please.	**Kan jag få notan, tack.**	kahn yaw foh NOH-tahn tack

*Swedish has various ways to say "please," depending on the context. The simplest is *snälla*, but Swedes sometimes use the word *tack* (thank you) in the way we use "please."

INDEX

INDEX

INDEX

Audio Europe

Rick's free app and podcasts

The FREE Rick Steves Audio Europe™ app for iPhone, iPad, iPod Touch and Android gives you self-guided audio tours of Europe's top museums, sights and historic walks—plus hundreds of tracks filled with cultural insights and sightseeing tips from Rick's radio interviews—all organized into geographic-specific playlists.

Let Rick Steves Audio Europe™ amplify your guidebook. This free app includes self-guided audio tours for all the most important museums and historical walks in London, Paris, Rome, Venice, Florence, Athens, and more.

With Rick whispering in your ear, Europe gets even better.

Thanks Facebook fans for submitting photos while on location! From top: John Kuijper in Florence, Brenda Mamer with her mother in Rome, and Alyssa Passey with her friend in Paris.

Find out more at ricksteves.com

Start your trip at

Free information and great gear to

▶ Plan Your Trip

Browse thousands of articles and a wealth of money-saving tips for planning your dream trip. You'll find up-to-date information on Europe's best destinations, packing smart, getting around, finding rooms, staying healthy, avoiding scams and more.

▶ Eurail Passes

Find out, step-by-step, if a railpass makes sense for your trip—and how to avoid buying more than you need. Get free shipping on online orders

▶ Graffiti Wall & Travelers Helpline

Learn, ask, share—our online community of savvy travelers is a great resource for first-time travelers to Europe, as well as seasoned pros.

Rick Steves' Europe Through the Back Door, Inc.

ricksteves.com

turn your travel dreams into affordable reality

▶ Free Audio Tours & Travel Newsletter

Get your nose out of this guide book and focus on what you'll be seeing with Rick's free audio tours of the greatest sights in Paris, London, Rome, Florence, Venice, and Athens.

Subscribe to our free Travel News e-newsletter, and get monthly articles from Rick on what's happening in Europe.

▶ Great Gear from Rick's Travel Store

Pack light and right—on a budget—with Rick's custom-designed carry-on bags, roll-aboards, day packs, travel accessories, guidebooks, journals, maps and DVDs of his TV shows.

130 Fourth Avenue North, PO Box 2009 • Edmonds, WA 98020 USA
Phone: (425) 771-8303 • Fax: (425) 771-0833 • www.ricksteves.com

Rick Steves

EUROPE GUIDES

Best of Europe
Eastern Europe
Europe Through the Back Door
Mediterranean Cruise Ports

COUNTRY GUIDES

Croatia & Slovenia
England
France
Germany
Great Britain
Ireland
Italy
Portugal
Scandinavia
Spain
Switzerland

CITY & REGIONAL GUIDES

Amsterdam, Bruges & Brussels
Budapest
Florence & Tuscany
Greece: Athens & the Peloponnese
Istanbul
London
Paris
Prague & the Czech Republic
Provence & the French Riviera
Rome
Venice
Vienna, Salzburg & Tirol

SNAPSHOT GUIDES

Barcelona
Berlin
Bruges & Brussels
Copenhagen & the Best of
    Denmark
Dublin
Dubrovnik
Hill Towns of Central Italy
Italy's Cinque Terre
Krakow, Warsaw & Gdansk
Lisbon
Madrid & Toledo
Munich, Bavaria & Salzburg
Naples & the Amalfi Coast
Northern Ireland
Norway
Scotland
Sevilla, Granada & Southern Spain
Stockholm

POCKET GUIDES

Athens
London
Paris
Rome

TRAVEL CULTURE

Europe 101
European Christmas
Postcards from Europe
Travel as a Political Act

NOW AVAILABLE:
eBOOKS, APPS & BLU-RAY

eBOOKS

Most guides are available as eBooks from Amazon, Barnes & Noble, Borders, Apple, and Sony. Free apps for eBook reading are available in the Apple App Store and Android Market, and eBook readers such as Kindle, Nook, and Kobo all have free apps that work on smartphones.

RICK STEVES' EUROPE DVDs

10 New Shows 2011–2012
Austria & the Alps
Eastern Europe
England & Wales
European Christmas
European Travel Skills & Specials
France
Germany, BeNeLux & More
Greece & Turkey
Iran
Ireland & Scotland
Italy's Cities
Italy's Countryside
Scandinavia
Spain
Travel Extras

BLU-RAY

Celtic Charms
Eastern Europe Favorites
European Christmas
Italy Through the Back Door
Mediterranean Mosaic
Surprising Cities of Europe

PHRASE BOOKS & DICTIONARIES

French
French, Italian & German
German
Italian
Portuguese
Spanish

JOURNALS

Rick Steves' Pocket Travel Journal
Rick Steves' Travel Journal

APPS

Select Rick Steves guides are available as apps in the Apple App Store.

PLANNING MAPS

Britain, Ireland & London
Europe
France & Paris
Germany, Austria & Switzerland
Ireland
Italy
Spain & Portugal

Rick Steves books and DVDs are available at bookstores and through online booksellers.

Avalon Travel
a member of the Perseus Books Group
1700 Fourth Street
Berkeley, CA 94710

Printed in the USA by Worzalla. First printing March 2012.

ISBN 978-1-61238-199-2

For the latest on Rick's lectures, guidebooks, tours, public radio show, and public television
series, contact Europe Through the Back Door, Box 2009, Edmonds, WA 98020, 425/771-
8303, fax 425/771-0833, www.ricksteves.com, rick@ricksteves.com.

Europe Through the Back Door Reviewers: Risa Laib, Jennifer Madison Davis
ETBD Editors: Tom Griffin, Suzanne Kotz, Cathy McDonald, Cathy Lu
Research Assistance: Tom Griffin, Cameron Hewitt, Ian Watson, Amanda Zurita
Avalon Travel Senior Editor and Series Manager: Madhu Prasher
Avalon Travel Project Editor: Kelly Lydick
Copy Editor: Rebecca Freed
Proofreader: Kyana Moghadam
Indexer: Stephen Callahan
Production & Typesetting: McGuire Barber Design
Cover Design: Kimberly Glyder Design
Graphic Content Director: Laura VanDeventer
Maps and Graphics: David C. Hoerlein, Laura VanDeventer, Twozdai Hulse, Lauren
  Mills, Kat Bennett, Mike Morgenfeld, Chris Markiewicz, Brice Ticen, Lohnes &
  Wright, Albert Angulo, Hank Evans
Photography: Cameron Hewitt, Sonja Groset, Rick Steves, Ian Watson, Tom Griffin,
  David C. Hoerlein, Dominic Bonuccelli, Lauren Mills, Renee Van Drent, Chris Werner
Cover Photo: Soder Malarstrand at Dawn, Stockholm, Sweden © Jon Arnold Images Ltd/
  Alamy

ABOUT THE AUTHOR

RICK STEVES

 Since 1973, Rick Steves has spent 100 days every year exploring Europe. Rick produces a public television series (*Rick Steves' Europe*), a public radio show (*Travel with Rick Steves*), and an app and podcast (*Rick Steves Audio Europe*); writes a bestselling series of guidebooks and a nationally syndicated newspaper column; organizes guided tours that take over ten thousand travelers to Europe annually; and offers an information-packed website (www.ricksteves.com). With the help of his hardworking staff of 80 at Europe Through the Back Door—in Edmonds, Washington, just north of Seattle—Rick's mission is to make European travel fun, affordable, and culturally enlightening for Americans.

More for your trip!
Maximize the experience with Rick Steves as your guide

Guidebooks
Dozens of European country and city guidebooks

Planning Maps
Use the map that's in sync with your guidebook

Rick's DVDs
Preview where you're going with 6 shows on Scandinavia

Free! Rick's Audio Europe™ App
Hear Scandinavia travel tips from Rick's radio shows

Small-Group Tours
Take a lively Rick Steves tour through Scandinavia

For all the details, visit ricksteves.com